Understanding Post-9/11 Afghanistan

A Critical Insight into Huntington's Civilizational Approach

DEEPSHIKHA SHAHI

E-INTERNATIONAL
RELATIONS
PUBLISHING

E-International Relations
www.E-IR.info
Bristol, England
2017

ISBN 978-1-910814-25-3 (paperback)
ISBN 978-1-910814-26-0 (e-book)

Production: Michael Tang
Copy Editing: Scot Purvis
Cover Image: Veneratio via Depositphotos

A catalogue record for this book is available from the British Library

E-IR Open Access

Series Editor: Stephen McGlinchey
Editorial Assistance: Johannes Grow & Brett Netto

E-IR Open Access is a series of scholarly books presented in a format that preferences brevity and accessibility while retaining academic conventions. Each book is available in print and e-book, and is published under a Creative Commons CC BY-NC 4.0 license. As E-International Relations is committed to open access in the fullest sense, free electronic versions of all of our books, including this one, are available on the E-International Relations website.

Find out more at: http://www.e-ir.info/publications

Recent titles

International Relations

Time, Temporality and Global Politics

Environment, Climate Change and International Relations

Ukraine's Euromaidan

System, Society and the World: Exploring the English School of International Relations (Second Edition)

About E-International Relations

E-International Relations is the world's leading open access website for students and scholars of international politics, reaching over three million readers per year. E-IR's daily publications feature expert articles, blogs, reviews and interviews – as well as student learning resources. The website is run by a non-profit organisation based in Bristol, England and staffed by an all-volunteer team of students and scholars.

http://www.e-ir.info

Abstract

9/11 and the subsequent war on terror have misleadingly reinforced the idea of a world politics based on a 'civilizational' clash. While post-9/11 Afghan society appears to be troubled with a conflict between so-called Islamic-terrorist and secular-democratic forces, the need for an alternative understanding to pave the way for peace has become paramount. This book uses a critical theoretical perspective to highlight the hidden political and economic factors underlying the so-called civilizational conflict in post-9/11 Afghanistan. It further demonstrates how a post-Islamic humanist discourse has the potential to not only carve the way for peace amidst dangerous entanglement between politics and religion in post-9/11 Afghanistan, but also vindicate Islam of its unjustified denigration in the contemporary world.

Deepshikha Shahi is Assistant Professor of Political Science at University of Delhi, India. She is set to pursue post-doctoral research at the Centre for Global Cooperation Research (Käte Hamburger-Kolleg), University of Duisburg-Essen, Germany. She is also affiliated with International Democracy Watch in Italy and Transnational Institute in Amsterdam. Her recent publications include 'Engaging with the post-secular moment in post-9/11 Afghanistan: the search for a "humanist" political discourse', *Cambridge Review of International Affairs* and 'Rethinking the absence of post-Western International Relations theory in India: "Advaitic monism" as an alternative epistemological resource', *European Journal of International Relations*.

Acknowledgements

My first and most earnest acknowledgement goes to Professor Achin Vanaik. Nearly six years ago, his magic in the classroom made Theory of International Relations fascinating for me and set me on the path I travelled at Delhi University. Professor Vanaik has been instrumental in ensuring my academic, professional and moral wellbeing ever since. In every sense, none of this work would have been possible without him. He has my sincere gratitude.

I also owe a huge debt of thankfulness to my friend Matilde Adduci, a Post-Doctoral Research Fellow at University of Turin and the Coordinator of the Summer School *TOIndia* at the Torino World Affairs Institute. She introduced me to Selay Gaffar, the Director of Humanitarian Assistance for the Women and Children of Afghanistan (HAWCA), a Kabul-based NGO. I am highly grateful to Selay and her team in Kabul who were immensely helpful in arranging my visit to their country and in organising my numerous illuminating interviews with Kabul-based diplomats, politicians, UN officials, American and European volunteers associated with INGOs, activists, social-workers, journalists, academicians and laymen. I thank Andeisha Farid, the Director of Afghan Child Education and Care Organization (AFCECO), another Kabul-based NGO, for providing logistical support in Kabul. Najib deserves particular credit for rendering his services as an interpreter during the interviews.

Besides Professor Vanaik's personal library, the valuable resources for this study were drawn from the Central Reference Library (CRL), Ratan Tata Library (RTL), and library of the Department of Political Science in Delhi University, Jawaharlal Nehru University Library, Teen Murti Library and the Institute for Defence Studies and Analyses (IDSA) Library. I am grateful to the staff of these libraries for their cooperation.

Any errors and unanswered questions remain mine. I stay especially appreciative of my friends Manashi and Vinay for patiently listening to my ideas and offering occasional intellectual inputs. My final and deepest acknowledgement goes to Dhiraj and my family for unconditionally trusting and encouraging me through all my ventures. For all that I am and for all that I am not, they have my everlasting love.

Contents

For Achin

1

Introduction

In the emerging world of ethnic conflict and civilizational clash, Western belief in the universality of Western culture suffers three problems: it is false; it is immoral; and it is dangerous.

(Samuel P. Huntington, 1996, p. 310)

Civilization as a significant unit of analysis and locus of debate in contemporary International Relations is largely an intellectual contribution of Samuel P. Huntington. His celebrated and controversial article and book about 'civilizations' (1993, 1996) have become some of the most widely quoted and translated analyses of the post-Cold War international order. Huntington had predicted a *civilizational turn* in post-Cold War world politics. In his bold rendering, civilizations were primeval entities that would replace ideology and geopolitics as the animating sources of cooperation and conflict in the post-Cold War world.[1] Huntington warned:

In the post-Cold War world flags count and so do other symbols of cultural identity, including crosses, crescents, and even head coverings, because culture counts, and cultural identity is what is most meaningful to most people. People are discovering new but often old identities and marching under new but often old flags which lead to wars with new but often old enemies... There can be no true friends without true enemies. Unless we hate what we are not, we cannot love what we are...The unfortunate truth in these old truths cannot be ignored by statesmen and scholars. For peoples seeking identity and reinventing ethnicity, enemies are essential, and

---

[1] According to Huntington, civilization means 'the highest cultural grouping of people and the broadest level of cultural identity people have short of that which distinguishes humans from other species.' See Huntington, Samuel Summer 1993, "The Clash of Civilizations?," *Foreign Affairs*, Vol. 72, No. 3, p. 24.

the potentially most dangerous enmities occur across the fault lines between the world's major civilizations.[2]

Huntington's attempt to provide a new mental map for perceiving the transformed 'civilizational' realities of post-Cold War world politics, led to the generation of two critical by-products: first, the *lofty picture of Western civilization*; second, the *tarnished image of Islam*. What has euphemistically, and possibly prematurely, been termed the 'New World Order' in the years following the collapse of the Soviet Union, has been idealised by references to a supposed superiority of Western civilization – its vision of humankind, including human rights and the economic and political system of liberalism. Huntington wrote: 'The West won the world not by the superiority of its ideas or values or religion, but rather by its superiority in applying organized violence.'[3]

A similar sentiment was echoed in the writings of Victor Davis Hanson. He asserted that there was a Western way of war, which because of certain features of Western civilization, had always been superior to non-Western ways, giving Westerners great military advantage. These features were generally derived from the Greek tradition and included concepts like limited government, civic participation, freedom of speech, critical inquiry, personal rights, and basic egalitarianism. According to him, these concepts produced superior aspects of Western war including massive formations like phalanxes and legions, as well as brutally annihilative tactics and goals.[4] Western scholars generally took great pride in their civilization which they claimed to be 'mightier' than other civilizations in both ideational and material senses.

The Western scholarly inclination for an inflated presentation of their 'civilizational' background was readily internalised and endorsed by Western leaders. A few days after 9/11, the Italian Prime Minister, Silvio Berlusconi, boasted of the supremacy of Western civilization by making the following controversial statement at a press conference:

> We should be conscious of the superiority of our civilization, which consists of a value system that has given people widespread prosperity in those countries that embrace it, and

[2] Huntington, Samuel P. 1997 *The Clash of Civilizations and the Remaking of World Order,* Simon and Schuster, p.20.
[3] Huntington, Samuel P. 1996 *The Clash of Civilizations and the Remaking of World Order*, Penguin, p. 51.
[4] Hanson, Victor Davis 2001 *Carnage and Culture: Landmark Battles in the Rise of Western Power*, Anchor Books.

guarantees respect for human rights and religion. This respect certainly does not exist in the Islamic countries.[5]

In the post-9/11 world, 'civilization' has filled the vacuum left by religion in the West's secularised environment. Western civilisation has emerged as an exemplar that is to be emulated either by will or by force. The norms inherent in the 'Western' way of life, of which the US is the epitome, have increasingly become the bases of legitimacy for economic and military policies across the globe.

On the flip side of this exalted status of the West, a myth pertaining to the dichotomy of good and evil has been deliberately produced, the most pronounced manifestation of which is the construct of the 'axis of evil.' This term was often used by US President George W. Bush to describe governments that he accused of harbouring terrorists *and seeking weapons of mass destruction.* The 'good' embodied in Western civilization has been highlighted in contrast to the alleged 'evil' intrinsic to Islam. Huntington's assertions were in line with the Western scholarly tradition of denouncing Islam:

> Islam's borders are bloody and so are its innards. The fundamental problem for the West is not Islamic fundamentalism. It is Islam, a different civilization whose people are convinced of the superiority of their culture and are obsessed with the inferiority of their power.[6]

Alexis de Tocqueville, for instance, had commented:

> I studied the Koran a great deal...I came away from that study with the conviction that by and large there have been few religions in the world as deadly to men as that of Muhammad. As far as I can see, it is the principal cause of the decadence so visible today in the Muslim world, and, though less absurd than the polytheism of old, its social and political tendencies are in my opinion infinitely more to be feared, and I therefore regard it as a form of decadence rather than a form of progress.[7]

[5]   Hooper, John and Connolly, Kate September 27, 2001 'Berlusconi Breaks Ranks Over Islam', *The Guardian,* available at http://www.guardian.co.uk/world/2001/sep/27/afghanistan.terrorism7
[6]   Huntington, Samuel P. 1996 *The Clash of Civilizations and the Remaking of World Order*, Penguin, p. 217.
[7]   Benoit Jean-Louis 2007 Notes sur le Coran et Autres Textes sur les Religions (Notes

Likewise, John Wesley said:

> Ever since the religion of Islam appeared in the world, the
> espousers of it...have been as wolves and tigers to all other
> nations, rending and tearing all that fell into their merciless
> paws, and grinding them with their iron teeth; that numberless
> cities are raised from the foundation, and only their name
> remaining; that many countries, which were once as the
> garden of God, are now a desolate wilderness; and that so
> many once numerous and powerful nations are vanished from
> the earth! Such was, and is at this day, the rage, the fury, the
> revenge, of these destroyers of human kind.[8]

It was believed in Western scholarly circles that the inferiority of Islam in
comparison to Western civilization chiefly emanated from its failure to blend
'reason' with 'faith'.

Ernest Volkman wrote:

> 'The Christian philosopher Thomas Aquinas described
> "reason" as the "bride of faith"'. Aquinas' idea that science, or
> rational inquiry into the laws of nature, could coexist with
> religion, was accepted by Western Civilization. In contrast, at
> the very moment Aquinas was telling his fellow Europeans how
> faith and reason could coexist, his Iranian counterpart, the
> Arab philosopher Ghazzali, concluded that the treasure of
> ancient texts represented social dynamite. The study of
> science and philosophy, he wrote, was harmful because it
> would shake man's faith in God and undermine the Muslim
> religion.[9]

To a great extent, the unscientific nature of Islamic faith was held responsible
for the backwardness of Muslim societies. Beyond Western scholars, some
Western leaders also express similar viewpoints. Taking an early example,
Winston Churchill once said:

---

on the Koran and Other Texts on Religion) by Alexis de Tocqueville, Bayard; reviewed
by Mazel, Michelle 2007 *Jewish Political Studies Review,* Vol. 19, pp. 3-4.

[8]   Blanton, Stephen 2011 *The Heart of Islam,* Author House, p.xxi-xxii.

[9]   Volkman, Ernest 2002 *Science Goes to War: The Search for the Ultimate Weapon,
from Greek Fire to Star Wars*, Wiley, p.60.

> How dreadful are the curses which Mohammedanism lays on its votaries! Besides the fanatical frenzy, which is as dangerous in a man as hydrophobia in a dog, there is this fearful fatalistic apathy. The effects are apparent in many countries. Improvident habits, slovenly systems of agriculture, sluggish methods of commerce, and insecurity of property exist wherever the followers of the Prophet rule or live... Far from being moribund, Mohammedanism is a militant and proselytizing faith.[10]

In the aftermath of 9/11, George W. Bush and Tony Blair tried to be politically correct by making rhetorical statements about the appreciable credentials of Islam. However, they have frequently vilified Islam by publicly defining criteria for its 'genuine' interpretation.[11] The over-simplified attribution of almost all post-9/11 terrorist activities to Islamic maxims has resulted in a distorted image of Islam, that in turn is being used to justify the 'civilizing mission' underlying the post-9/11 US-led global war on terrorism.

9/11 has demonstrated how the world's only superpower is not immune from the dangers and fragility of the current international system. A decade after 9/11, the ranking Republican on the Intelligence Committee, Senator Richard Shelby, said: 'If there was any certainty in the weeks and months after the 9/11 attacks, it was that these were just the first in a campaign of terror on American soil. You can just about bet on it'.[12] The Chairman of the 9/11 Commission, Thomas Kean, expressed a similar apprehension at the Bipartisan Policy Center in Washington D.C. He stated: 'We are safer but we are not as secure yet as we can or should be'.[13] Emphasising the political discomfort caused by post-9/11 wars, George Will wrote: 'Today, for reasons having little do with 9/11 and policy responses to it, the nation is more demoralized than at any time since the late 1970s, when, as now, feelings of

---

[10] Churchill, Winston 1899 *The River War* available at http://www.freerepublic.com/focus/f-news/1575199/posts

[11] See Pipes, Daniel 26 November 2001 'What's True Islam?: Not for U.S. to Say', *New York Post*; Sutton, Philip W. and Vertigans, Stephen 2005 *Resurgent Islam: A Sociological Approach*, Polity, p.150; Besteman, Lowe and Gusterson 2005 *Why America's Top Pundits are Wrong*, University of California Press, pp. 36-42.

[12] Chapman, Steve September 8, 2011 'Who Kept Us Safe After 9/11?', *Chicago Tribune,* available at http://articles.chicagotribune.com/2011-09-08/news/ct-oped-0908-chapman-20110908_1_terrorist-attacks-car-bomb-domestic-terrorism

[13] Mintz, Elianna August 31, 2011 '9/11 Commission Warns U.S. Still Vulnerable 10 Years After Attacks', *The Talk Radio News Service,* available at http://www.talkradionews.com/news/2011/8/31/9-11-commission-warns-us-still-vulnerable-10-years-after-att.html

impotence, vulnerability, and decline were pervasive'.[14]

While 9/11 exposed the vulnerability of the US on the one hand, it seriously questioned the ethical premises of US foreign policy, especially towards Afghanistan, Iraq and the Middle East, on the other. Stephen Eric Bronner wrote: 'American foreign policy in the aftermath of 9/11 has increasingly been associated with the use of a double standard by much of the world'.[15] Joan Hoff critiqued post-9/11 US foreign policy by showing how moralistic diplomacy had increasingly taken on Faustian overtones. She argued that as long as the ideological outcome of the Cold War remained in doubt, there was little reason for presidents or government decision-makers to question the unethical aspects of US relations with the rest of the world or the universal and exceptional nature of American values. 9/11 allowed the US to assert its exceptionalism and dominance more unilaterally than ever before.[16] Not surprisingly, discussion of Huntington's clash of civilizations thesis has frequently taken place in post-9/11 debates. Nevertheless, a simplistic understanding of 9/11 and the subsequent US-led war on terror in Afghanistan as exemplifications of a clash of civilizations seems to be thoroughly misleading and dangerous. It is misleading as it omits various crucial factors that refute the applicability of Huntington's thesis in the context of post-9/11 Afghanistan. It is dangerous as it reinforces the overly elevated status of the West in comparison to a maligned portrait of Islam, thereby provoking violent exchanges between the fanatic sympathisers of the two 'civilizations'.

A sincere attempt to check this misleading and dangerous tendency requires an alternative understanding of the post-9/11 Afghan scenario that may serve the following objectives: (i) Expose the theoretical loopholes and practical pitfalls implicit in Huntington's thesis of civilizational clash; (ii) Explain the popular receptivity of Huntington's thesis despite its inadequacies; (iii) Reveal the hidden political motives of the West behind projecting Islam as an evil force, particularly in relation to the war on terror in Afghanistan; (iv) Diagnose the historical and sociological roots of the post-9/11 Afghan conflict; and (v) Suggest a way out of the ongoing crisis facing Afghanistan, in particular, and Islam, in general.

---

[14] Will, George September 11, 2011 '9/11, Wars Leave the US Feeling Vulnerable', *Newsmax*, available at http://www.newsmax.com/GeorgeWill/9-11-iraq/2011/09/11/id/410468

[15] Bronner, Stephen Eric 2011 'On Judging American Foreign Policy: Human Rights, Political Realism and the Arrogance of Power', *Logos: A Journal of Modern Society and Culture*, available at http://logosjournal.com/2011/summer_bronner/

[16] Hoff, Joan 2007 *A Faustian Foreign Policy from Woodrow Wilson to George W. Bush: Dreams of Perfectibility,* Cambridge University Press.

This study undertakes the responsibility of fulfilling the above-mentioned objectives by adopting two theoretical strategies: first, evoking the academic discipline of psychology to grasp the interface between aggressive scripts and violent acts[17]; second, employing the alternative framework of *Critical International Theory* (CIT), developed by Robert W. Cox and Andrew Linklater, and inspired by the works of Antonio Gramsci and Jurgen Habermas respectively, to decode and propose a settlement of post-9/11 Afghan crisis. The study raises the following central question: Do the paradigms offered by CIT – namely 'production' and 'communication' – prove more effective in terms of their descriptive, explanatory and emancipatory capacity, than the paradigm offered by the clash of civilizations thesis in portraying post-9/11 Afghanistan?

An appropriate response to this central question demands attention to several related questions:

- What are the basic propositions of the clash of civilizations thesis?
- Can we see the 9/11 attacks and the subsequent US-led war on terror in Afghanistan as the prelude to a renewed clash of civilizations?
- Does the case of post-9/11 Afghan politics fit into the frame of the civilizational conflict paradigm?
- What are the gaps in the clash of civilizations thesis that lead to its failure in providing an adequate portrayal of post-9/11 Afghanistan?
- How are these gaps exposed and filled up by taking a critical-theoretical standpoint?
- How can CIT provide an alternative understanding of post-9/11 Afghanistan?
- Can CIT offer a practical agenda to transform the post-9/11 Afghan crisis?

The study examines these questions against the following hypothesis: the dual paradigms offered by CIT can be effectively utilised for serving a twofold purpose – first, highlighting the hidden political and economic factors underlying the so-called civilizational conflict in post-9/11 Afghanistan; second, revealing the implications of distortions in the 'civilizational' dialogue for determining the dynamics of post-9/11 Afghan politics. This twofold approach can facilitate a critical appraisal of the clash of civilizations thesis as well as suggest an apt way of addressing and transforming the post-9/11 Afghan crisis.

---

[17] Although most researchers focus on the use of aggressive scripts by delinquents, the scripts are as available for use in international conflicts, in bullying and gang wars. See Millon, Theodore 2003 *Handbook of Psychology: Personality and Social Psychology*, Volume 5, Wiley, p. 571.

The methodology of the study is textual, comparative, analytical, interdisciplinary, post-positivist and emancipatory. It relies on various texts – books, articles, interviews, reports, statements, speeches, and agreements – for empirical support. It compares the effectiveness and utility of the clash of civilizations thesis to that of CIT. It analyses the political developments in post-9/11 Afghanistan by taking various theoretical standpoints. It merges the insights gained from psychology with International Relations theory. It endorses the post-positivist view that the notion of truth/reality created by the positivist clash of civilizations thesis is formed from a certain perspective and for some purpose which can be interpreted by tracing its political consequences. It takes the path of self-reflection to perceive the Afghan society as a site of power-struggles and demonstrates the historical compulsions of the past which constrain its emancipation while simultaneously possessing the potential for its realisation.

The primary sources consulted in the study include a series of interviews with Kabul-based diplomats, politicians, UN officials, American and European volunteers associated with INGOs, activists, social-workers, journalists, academicians, and laymen. These interviews were conducted during the author's visit to Kabul in July 2011. Though the data collected through these interviews do not correspond to a fully-fledged empirical method normally associated with standard 'quantitative' field studies, the data nonetheless remain illustrative, authentic and vital primarily for their 'qualitative' value as these were produced by individuals on behalf of their respective organisations. The pen-portraits and organisation profiles of these individuals and the sample questionnaire used for conducting the interviews have been provided in the appendixes.

The study is divided into four chapters. Chapter 2 lays out the origin and character of Huntington's thesis and categorises its various criticisms under three heads – epistemological, methodological, and ethical. Since the existing criticisms are weak when it comes to explaining the widespread receptivity of Huntington's thesis, the chapter turns to the 'humanistic-existential model' of psychology for designing a 'psychological critique' of the clash of civilizations thesis, thereby explaining the popular receptivity of Huntington's thesis and suggesting a nexus between 'knowledge' and 'violence.'

Chapter 3 reveals the specific historical factors that refute the applicability of Huntington's thesis to 9/11 and the subsequent US-led war on terrorism in Afghanistan. However, the chapter argues that the inapplicability of Huntington's thesis does not automatically imply the absence of the popularity of Huntington's thesis in Afghanistan. The chapter sets out to examine the general history of 'political reception' in Afghan politics, thereby explaining the popular receptivity of Huntington amongst the Afghans, on the one hand, and exposing the harmful impact of Huntington's ideas on post-9/11 Afghan politics, on the other.

Chapter 2 uses the humanistic-existential model of psychology to challenge the theoretical authenticity of Huntington's thesis, whereas Chapter 3 throws light on the myriad complexities of post-9/11 Afghanistan to raise questions about the analytical potential of Huntington's thesis. However, the task of highlighting flaws in Huntington's thesis is not as significant and desirable as discovering an alternative theoretical framework that is more meritorious in terms of its capability to comprehend social reality. Chapter 4 attempts to establish Critical International Theory (CIT) as a more meritorious theoretical framework than Huntington's thesis. It constructs CIT as a single overarching framework, traces the overlap between the assertions of CIT and the humanistic-existential model of psychology, and demonstrates the relative strengths of CIT against the weaknesses of the clash of civilizations thesis. In general, CIT is often viewed not as an integral whole but as an amalgam of two distinct paradigms concerning two distinct concepts and processes. The production paradigm tends to focus on the concept of work and struggles over redistribution. The communication paradigm is concerned with the concept of interaction and identity struggles. Critics argue that neither paradigm is adequate for the task of understanding the problematic of the other. They hold that the 'work-interaction divide' is the fundamental problem of CIT. However, this study tries its best to counter this charge. It sets out to forge a strong nexus between the twin paradigms of CIT. The study asserts that the common emancipatory objective of the dual paradigms of CIT emanates from a common broad intellectual project wherein the themes of *hegemony*, *reason* and *transcendence* play a central role.

Chapter 5 aims at providing an alternative and comparatively more accurate understanding of post-9/11 Afghanistan by applying the dual paradigms of CIT. The alternative understanding reconstructs the post-9/11 Afghan scenario as an instance of clash of hegemonic aspirations. The chapter demonstrates that the shifting of perspective from 'civilizational' to 'critical' not only presents a finer vision of the post-9/11 Afghan crisis but also suggests a way out of it. In its effort to find a solution to the troubling state of affairs in post-9/11 Afghanistan, it explores the possibility of organising an effective 'counter-hegemonic struggle' that in turn would require designing an 'alternative knowledge-base', organising the critical social forces along 'alternative social relations of production', and creating an 'all-inclusive speech community.' The chapter finally toys with the idea of a 'humanistic re-interpretation of Quran' which might not only pave the way for transforming the post-9/11 Afghan crisis but also prove to be a decisive step towards redeeming Islam from both Muslim and non-Muslim extremists who project themselves as contenders for global hegemony in the contemporary world.

One of the intentions behind undertaking this study is to respond to those critics who disapprove of critical theorists for not developing testable theories. Robert O. Keohane, for instance, admits that the 'reflectivist' stance of critical theorists promises significant insights into the intersubjective bases of international relations, particularly institutional construction. He, however, laments that critical theorists have been more adept at pointing out what is omitted in rationalistic theory than in developing theories of their own with a priori content. He reiterates with Judith Goldstein that supporters of critical theory need to develop 'testable theories' and to be explicit about their scope.[18] By testing the theoretical assertions of CIT against the practical evidence drawn from post-9/11 Afghan politics, this study attempts to highlight the methodological edges of CIT over and above the traditional/rationalistic theories of International Relations.

Another motivating factor underlying this study is to demonstrate the reformative potential of CIT. Andrew Linklater lays emphasis upon the 'praxeological question of reform' which is best addressed by CIT.

He opines that 'due to the dominance of the realist emphasis on international systemic constraints on the tension between power and morality, and on the dangers of idealist praxeology, the question of how states and other social actors could create new political communities and identities has never been adequately addressed. Providing an adequate answer is a central requirement for the critical theory of international relations'.[19]

Likewise, Raymond Duvall and Latha Varadarajan argue that CIT shares a commitment to challenging the naturalness of the existing world order and the acceptability of its dominant relations and practices of power. They write:

> Critical theory analyses the effects of power and the differential ability of actors to control their own circumstances. It also goes beyond that theoretical contribution to provide impetus for practical political action in challenging, confronting, and disrupting existing relations of power. Thus, in the contemporary era, critical IR theory is relevant, among other ways, as a stimulus to resist empire in its many guises.[20]

---

[18] Linklater, Andrew 2000 *International Relations: Critical Concepts in Political Science,* Volume 4, Routledge, p. 1789.

[19] Linklater, Andrew 1992 'The Question of the Next Stage in International Relations Theory', *Millennium*, Vol.21, No.1, p. 96.

[20] Duvall, Raymond and Varadarajan, Latha 2003 'On the Practical Significance of

The present study is an attempt to shed light on the desirable course of action for resisting the imperialist tendencies in post-9/11 Afghanistan.

A heavy 'theoretical' orientation for the most part of this study might raise scepticism with regard to its practical relevance. However, the study endorses an indivisible yet detached linkage between theory and the practice of politics which is arguably best captured in the following words of a critical theorist, Theodore W. Adorno:

> However inseparable these two distinct disciplines – theory and practice – may be, since after all they both have their source in life itself, there is one further factor necessary for practice that is not fully explicable by theory and that is very hard to isolate. And I should like to emphasise it because I regard it as fundamental to a definition of the moral...One task of the theory of the moral is to set limits to the scope of theory itself, in other words, to show that the sphere of moral action includes something that cannot fully be described in intellectual terms, but also that should not be turned into an absolute... I find it extraordinarily difficult to find words to describe this factor...But I believe that we found a clue to it... when I was telling you about the concept of resistance...when someone decides not to do anything for once, but to retreat from the dominant realm of practical activity in order to think about something essential. Now what I wish to emphasise is the factor of resistance, of refusing to be part of the prevailing evil, a refusal that always implies resisting something stronger and hence always contains an element of despair. I believe that this idea of resistance, then, may help you best to see what I mean when I say that the moral sphere is not coterminous with the theoretical sphere, and that this fact is itself a basic philosophical determinant of the sphere of practical action.[21]

This study can be considered a small effort towards touching that philosophical zone of morality that according to Adorno lies somewhere between, and yet beyond, the theoretical and practical reach of existence.

Critical International Relations Theory', *Asian Journal of Political Science,* Vol. 11, Issue 2, pp. 75-88.

[21] Adorno, Theodore W. 2001 *Problems of Moral Philosophy* edited by Thomas Schroder, translated by Rodney Livingstone, Stanford University Press, pp. 3-8.

2

The Clash of Civilizations Thesis: A Critical Appraisal

Theory and the "real world" constantly badger and hound each other, the former straining to corral the latter, and the latter racing away, producing a necessary tension in an "interactive" mode because both dimensions - the theoretical and the world it tries to represent - are dynamic.

(Michael P. Sullivan, 2001, p16.)

The tension between theory and the 'real world' can produce a tendency to see the development of theory as a response to events in the world, with seemingly new phenomena requiring fresh theories – the most recent phenomena involving the end of the Cold War, the demise of bipolarity, and questions about the status of American hegemony. The academic discipline of International Relations (IR) awaited a new paradigm which could provide an outlook to delineate the picture of the newly emerging world politics after the end of the Cold War. Interestingly, various contending paradigms cropped up, most of these originating in the West – particularly in the US. The linkage is in fact significant as it demonstrates the knowledge-power relationship in international relations. If the US could disguise its empire building project and legitimise its aggressive foreign policy behaviour as a necessary defensive posture to contain the threat of communism and the USSR during the Cold War, it could not continue to do so after the collapse of USSR and the end of the Cold War. It was, therefore, in greater need than ever before of the legitimising discourses that many North American and European intellectuals of the right and liberal centre seemed eager to provide.[22] Of these legitimising discourses the one that earned the most attention was that of Samuel P. Huntington's clash of civilizations thesis. In fact, the proponents and critics of his thesis have virtually created a 'clash of scholarship' in IR. This chapter

---
[22]   Vanaik, Achin, 2007 *Masks of Empire* Tulika Books, p2.

aims at demonstrating the various dimensions of this clash of scholarship whilst adding a new dimension to it. It consists of three sections. The first section attempts to lay out the origin and character of Huntington's thesis. The second section tries to categorise the various criticisms of it. Finally, the third section sets out to offer a psychological critique of the clash of civilizations thesis, thereby suggesting a nexus between 'knowledge' and 'violence'.

Sketching the Origin and Character

Huntington called forth a paradigmatic shift to comprehend post-Cold War global politics as he held that 'inter-civilizational' issues were replacing inter-superpower ones.[23] Huntington's clash of civilizations thesis endeavoured to offer a new paradigm of world politics, which in contrast to state-centric realist theory and the system dominated neo–realist model, focused on civilizational-cultural religious factors.[24] In his article, *The Clash of Civilizations?,* published in *Foreign Affairs* in Summer 1993 (later expanded in his 1996 book *The Clash of Civilizations and the Remaking of World Order*), he laid down his basic propositions:

> It is my hypothesis that the fundamental source of conflict in this new world will not be primarily ideological or primarily economic. The great divisions among humankind and the dominating source of conflict will be cultural. Nation States will remain the most powerful actors in world affairs but the principal conflicts of global politics will occur between nations and groups of different civilizations. The clash of civilizations will dominate global politics. The fault lines between civilizations will be battle lines of the future.[25]

Huntington claimed that the fault lines between civilizations stemmed from differences in social and political values. The civilizations had different values on the relations between God and man, the individual and group, the citizen and state, parents and children, husband and wife, as well as differing views of the relative importance of rights and responsibilities, liberty and authority,

---

[23] Huntington, Samuel P. November-December 1993 'If Not Civilizations, What?: Paradigms of the Post-Cold War World', *Foreign Affairs,* pp.187-189.

[24] Three years before the arrival of Huntington's thesis, Bernard Lewis talked about the clash of civilizations. See Lewis, Bernard September 1990 'The Roots of Muslim Rage: Why so many Muslims Deeply Resent the West and Why Their Bitterness Will Not be Easily Mollified' *The Atlantic Monthly,* Vol. 266, No. 3,pp 47-58.

[25] Huntington, Samuel P. Summer 1993 'The Clash of Civilizations?' *Foreign Affairs* Vol. 72, No. 3, pp. 21-49.

equality and hierarchy.[26] Most of the arguments in the pages that followed relied on a vague notion of something Huntington called 'civilization identity' and the interaction among seven or eight major 'civilizations' of which the conflict between two of them, 'Islam' and 'the West', got the lion's share of his attention.

The article's most controversial statement came when Huntington demonised Islam by suggesting a linkage between Islam and violence. He wrote,

> In Eurasia the great historic fault lines between civilizations are once more aflame. This is particularly true along the boundaries of the crescent shaped Islamic block of nations from the bulge of Africa to Central Asia. Violence also occurs between Muslims on the one hand, and orthodox Serbs in the Balkans, Jews in Israel, Hindus in India, Buddhists in Burma and Catholics in the Philippines. Islam has bloody borders.[27]

Huntington enumerated six causes of intra-Islamic and extra-Islamic violence. *Militarism, indigestibility*, or less adaptability, and *proximity to non-Muslim groups,* explained the Muslim conflict propensity throughout history while *anti-Muslim prejudice, absence of core state in Islam* and *demographic explosion in Muslim societies* were held responsible for Muslim violence in the late twentieth century.[28]

The most remarkable portion of Huntington's thesis dealt with policy recommendations. With regard to US domestic policy Huntington emphasised upon the need for tightening immigration and assimilating immigrants and minorities so as to increase civilizational coherence. He favoured Americanisation and denounced multiculturalism, as it weakened the American creed. Huntington's guidelines on US foreign policy pressed the importance of maintaining Western technological and military superiority over other civilizations, non-interference in the affairs of other civilizations, empowering Atlantic partnership between US and Europe, limiting the expansion of Islamic–Confucian states, and exploiting the difference between these two civilizations.[29] The provocative thoughts underlying Huntington's thesis drew massive criticism.

---

[26] Ibid.

[27] Huntington, Samuel P. Summer 1993 'The Clash of Civilizations?' *Foreign Affairs* Vol. 72, No. 3, pp. 21-49.

[28] Huntington, Samuel P. 1996, *The Clash of Civilizations and the Remaking of World Order*, Penguin, pp. 262-265.

[29] Huntington, Samuel P. November-December 1996 'The West Unique, Not Universal', *Foreign Affairs*, p. 45.

Categorising the Critique

The criticisms of the clash of civilizations thesis can categorised under three headings - epistemological, methodological and ethical. The epistemological critique condemns the clash of civilizations thesis on grounds of its realist, orientalist and elitist outlook. The methodological critique attacks its monolithic, inconsistent and reductionist/essentialist attitude while the ethical critique denounces it for being a purposeful thesis that fuels enemy discourse and, in the process, becomes a self-fulfilling prophecy.

Epistemological Critique

The epistemological critique problematises the very source of Huntington's thesis in three ways. Firstly, it claims that the clash of civilizations thesis does not come up with a new paradigm since it neatly fits into political realism.[30] Huntington's emphasis on the ever-present probability of war between civilizations represents a fear that is deeply rooted in political realism. The Machiavellian advice of Huntington to exploit the difference between Islamic and Confucian civilizations can only be considered within the realist realm.[31] According to Muhammad Asadi, the clash of civilizations thesis is dismantled historically as soon as we realise that it is nothing new. It is the same Cold War methodology rebranded for maximum impact, a contrived clash that the US was pursuing for several decades by converting an old ally into foe post-World War Two. This repackaging for a new era was necessary because the old enemy, the Soviet Union, no longer existed. Hans Kung contends that Huntington follows a bloc based Cold War mentality where war is considered crucial for maintaining the West's technological and military superiority.[32] In a similar vein, G. John Ikenberry, Rubenstein and Crocker assert that Huntington proclaims the slogan - *long live the Cold War!*[33]

Secondly, the epistemological critique argues that the clash of civilizations thesis is *orientalist.* It claims that the language of 'us' and 'them' is embedded in Huntington's thesis. Edward W. Said claims that the 'epistemology of othering' underlying Huntington's thesis is problematic as labels,

---

[30] Rubenstein, Richard E. and Crocker, Jarle 'Challenging Huntington' *Foreign Policy*, No. 96 (Fall, 1994),pp 115-117.

[31] Hussein, Seifudein Adem 2001 'On the End of History and the Clash of Civilizations: A Dissenter's View' *Journal of Muslim Minority Affairs*, Vol. 21, NO. 1, p. 32.

[32] Kung, Hans ' Inter-Cultural Dialogue Versus Confrontation' in Schmiegleow, Henrik (ed) 1999 *Preventing the Clash of Civilizations: A Peace Strategy for the Twenty-First Century,* St. Martin's Press, p 103.

[33] Ikenberry , G. John March-April 1997 'Just Like the Rest,' *Foreign Affairs*, p. 163 and Rubenstein, op.cit,p 117.

generalisations and cultural assertions are finally inadequate. He further argues that it is simpler to make bellicose statements for the purpose of mobilising collective passions than to reflect, examine, and sort out what it is we are dealing with in reality, the interconnectedness of innumerable lives, 'ours' as well as 'theirs'.[34] This oriental scholarship perceives Islam as a threat to the West.[35] The act of perceiving the 'other' as a 'threat' rather than a 'challenge' leads to a siege mentality generated by Western hubris.[36] Manochehr Dorraj raises objections over the reification, distortion and dehumanisation of the Muslims produced by the clash of civilizations thesis.[37] Said opines that the 'fictional gimmick' constructed by such an orientalist approach is better for reinforcing defensive self-pride than for any critical understanding of the bewildering interdependence of our time.

Thirdly, the epistemological critique finds fault with the elitist orientation of the clash of civilizations thesis. It argues that Huntington's thesis is an 'official mythology' generated by US elites to 'scare the hell out of the American people', as ex-US Senator Vanderbilt put it. Therefore, the agenda of US elites differs from that of the American masses. Interestingly, the clash of civilizations rhetoric is not limited to American and European elites - many al-Qaida militants also view the current US-led conflicts in the Middle East as proof of a clash between Islam and the West.[38] Oliver Roy admits that Huntington is regularly accused of having introduced the concept of the clash of civilizations, but this approach is also shared by fundamentalists and conservative Muslims.[39] Gilles Kepel points out that Ayman al-Zawahiri's text *Knights Under the Prophet's Banner* presents a worldview comparable, but in reverse, to Huntington's thesis. Zawahiri's book is a jihadist reading of the clash of civilizations.[40] These observations compelled Michael Dunn to conclude that the clash of civilizations is an essential form of discourse for two powerful groups of elites - the Western policymakers and the leaders of the al-Qaida network. Benjamin Barber further highlights the gap between the

---

[34] Said, op.cit.

[35] Monshipouri, Mahmood and Petonito, Gina Autumn1995 'Constructing the Enemy in the Post-Cold War Era: The Flaws of the Islamic Conspiracy Theory' *Journal of Church and State*, Vol. 37, No. 4, pp. 773-792.

[36] Mahbubani, Kishore Summer 1992 'The West and the Rest', *National Interest,* Issue 28, pp. 10-14.

[37] Dorraj, Manochehr December 1998, 'In the Throes of Civilizational Conflict', *Peace Review*, Vol. 10, No. 4, pp. 633-637.

[38] Dunn, Michael Winter 2006-2007 'The Clash of Civilizations and the War on Terror', *49th Parallel*, Vol. 20 available at http://www.49thparallel.bham.ac.uk/back/issue20/Dunn.pdf

[39] Roy, Oliver 2004 *Globalized Islam: The Search for a New Ummah,* Hurst and Company, p9.

[40] Kepel, Gilles 2004 *The War for Muslim Minds: Islam and the West,* Belknap Press, p99.

agenda of elites and masses in the Islamic world by stating that hyperbolic commentators like Huntington have described the current divide in the world as a clash of civilizations, but this is to ape the messianic rhetoric of Osama bin Laden, who called for precisely such a war. The difference between bin Laden's terrorists and the poverty-stricken constituents he tries to call to arms, however, is the difference between radical Jihadist elites and ordinary men and women concerned with feeding their children and nurturing their religious communities.[41] Thus, the real clash is not between the civilizations but between the elites and the masses over the definition of reality. Said calls it the 'clash of ignorance'.

Methodological Critique

The methodological critique condemns Huntington's thesis on three grounds. Firstly, it objects to the monolithic conception of civilizations which neglects the polycentric structure of both worlds.[42] Fred Halliday argues that Huntington ignores the internal dynamics, plurality and myriad complexities of Islam and the Muslim world.[43] Aijaz Ahmad asserts that there is no single Islamic culture, but multiple centres of Islam and various types of political Islam and Islamism in the Muslim world.[44] Ibrahim Kalin calls for deconstructing the monolithic perceptions of Islam and the West.[45] The existence of numerous conflicts within civilizations and cooperation between civilizations refutes the monolithic orientation of Huntington's thesis. For instance, M.E. Ahrari asks Huntington as to how Iraqi and Turkish treatment of Kurds can demonstrate civilizational unity and coherence?[46] Shireen T. Hunter cites the case of Turkey's strategic relations with Israel in the 1990s, when its relations with the Arab world and Iran were generally problematic.[47]

Secondly, the methodological critique pinpoints the inconsistencies in Huntington's thesis. It disagrees with the selective perception and

---

[41] Barber, Benjamin 2003 *Jihad vs. Mcworld*, Corgi, p.xv.
[42] See the book review of the Clash of Civilizations and the Remaking of World Order by Richard Rosecrance December 1998 *American Political Science Review*, Vol. 92, No. 4, p978-980.
[43] Halliday , Fred 1996 *Islam and the Myth of Confrontation*, St. Martin's Press,p 217.
[44] Ahmad, Aijaz 2008 'Islam, Islamisms and the West', *Socialist Register* available at http://www.iran-bulletin.org/political%20islam/SR_08_Ahmad_0.pdf
[45] Kalin, Ibrahim 2001 'Islam and the West: Deconstructing Monolithic Perceptions-A Conversation With Professor John Esposito' *Journal of Muslim Minority Affairs*, Vol. 21, No. 1, pp 155-163.
[46] Ahrari, M.E., Spring 1997 'The Clash of Civilizations: An Old Story or New Truth?', *New Perspectives Quarterly*, Vol. 14. No. 2, pp 56-61.
[47] Hunter, Shireen T. 1998 *The Future of Islam and the West: Clash of Civilizations or Peaceful Coexistence?*, Praeger, p 169.

overgeneralization involved in Huntington's reading of history. For instance, Fouad Ajami contends that the Gulf War is a case for 'clash of state interest' rather than 'clash of civilizations'.[48] Similarly Hunter criticises Huntington's portrayal of the Armenian–Azerbaijan conflict as a civilizational clash since Muslim Iran had more friendly relations with Christian Armenians, than with Muslim Azerbaijan. Robert Marks is dissatisfied with the fact that Huntington mostly uses secondary sources in his book and shows a weak scholarship of Islam, China, and Japan.[49] Seizaburo Sato raises objections over the illogicality of Huntington's thesis since he makes Russia the core state of Slavic Orthodox civilization yet advises that Russia should be brought into the EU. Sato further raises the question as to why Huntington suggests setting Japan against potential Islamic Confucian alignment, when he defines Japan as an economic threat to the West?[50] The critics find Huntington's thesis confusing as he uses the term 'religion', 'culture', and 'civilization' interchangeably.

Thirdly, the methodological critique attacks the reductionist / essentialist tone of the thesis in two senses: First, it reduces the multiple causes of inter-and intra-national conflict, thereby essentialising the civilizational factor as the prime reason. Second, it reduces the multiple dimensions of individual identity, thereby essentialising the civilizational factor as the chief aspect.

The scholars who refute the essentialisation of a civilizational cause of conflict include Noam Chomsky, Fouad Ajami, Shireen T. Hunter and James Kurth. Chomsky accepts that there is clash between 'the West' and 'the rest'. However, he opines that the West is in clash with those who are adopting the preferential option for the poor no matter who they are. They can be Catholics (in Latin America) or Communists (in Afghanistan). Chomsky refers to Charles Tilly to assert that over the last millennium,

> Western states have been ruthlessly at war because of a central tragic fact that coercion works. Those who apply substantial force to their fellows get compliance, and from that compliance draw multiple advantages of money, goods, deference, and access to pleasures denied to less powerful people.[51]

---

[48] Ajami, Fouad, September-October 1993 'The Summoning' *Foreign Affairs* Vol. 72, No. 4, pp 7-8.

[49] See the book review of The Clash of Civilizations and the Remaking of World Order by Robert Marks Spring 2002 *Journal of World History,* Vol. 11, No.1, pp101-104.

[50] Sato, Seizaburo October 1997 'The Clash of Civilizations: A View from Japan', *Asia Pacific Review* 4, pp. 7-23.

[51] Sridhar, V., November 24 - December 7 2001 'Chomsky in India', *Frontline,* Vol. 18,

Fouad Ajami complains that Huntington overestimates the cultural differences between civilizations and underestimates the influence of the West in hostile relations with the Muslim world. Shireen T. Hunter and Muhammad Asadi point out that the conflictive relations between the West and the Muslim world hardly stems from civilizational differences but from structural-political and economic inequalities between the two worlds of 'haves' and 'have nots'.[52] James Kurth presents a more complicated picture that the real clash is not between the West and the rest, as Huntington assumes, but between pro-Western conservatives and post-Western liberal multiculturalists in the West itself.[53]

The scholars who denounce the essentialisation of the civilizational aspect of individual identity include Amartya Sen and Achin Vanaik. Sen refuses it as it ignores the multiple dimensions of identity that overlap across the so-called civilizational boundaries, while Achin Vanaik rejects it as it overlooks the dynamic and historically contingent nature of the inter-relationship between civilization, culture, and identity. Sen, in his book *Identity and Violence: The Illusion of Destiny*, expresses the view that the difficulty with Huntington's approach begins with his system of unique categorization. He claims that the thesis of a civilizational clash is conceptually parasitic on the commanding power of a unique categorisation along so-called civilizational lines, which closely follows religious divisions, to which singular attention is paid. Sen warns that the increasing failure to acknowledge the many identities that any person has and to try to firmly place the individual into rigid boxes, essentially shaped by a pre-eminent religious identity, is an intellectual confusion that can cause dangerous divisiveness. An Islamist instigator of violence against infidels may want Muslims to forget that they have identities other than being Islamic. What is surprising for Sen is that those who would like to quell that violence promote, in effect, the same intellectual disorientation by seeing Muslims primarily as members of an Islamic world. According to Sen, the people of the world can be classified on the basis of many other partitions: nationalities, locations, classes, occupations, social status, languages, politics, and so on. Sen believes that the world is made much more incendiary by the single-dimensional categorisation of human beings, which combines haziness of vision with an increased scope for the exploitation of that haze by the champions of violence.

Achin Vanaik, in his book *The Furies of Indian Communalism*, provides a sophisticated understanding of the concept of 'civilization', 'culture', and

---

No. 24, available at http://www.frontline.in/static/html/fl1824/18240230.htm
[52] Hunter, op.cit, pp19-20.
[53] Kurth, James Summer 2001 'American and the West: Global Triumph or Western Twilight ?', *Orbis*, pp. 333-341.

'identity' as against the over-simplistic notions entertained by Huntington. He accounts for two types of civilizational studies. The first is a transhistorical and culturally essentialist reading of the enduring impact of some initial civilizational entity or root. The second is a historically well rounded study where civilization is seen as a network of specific historical, geographical, economic, political, cultural and social complexes, and not primarily as transhistorical cultural complexes. Such civilizations follow the pattern of emergence, rise, decline, and fall. In such an approach, it is difficult to talk – as Huntington does – of any specific civilization, let alone of many such civilizations existing through millennia.[54]

Vanaik further argues that the concept of culture bears a dual connotation – essence and process.[55] Many a twentieth century civilization theorist of Weberian cast saw civilizations as 'cultural visions' that have soul, spirit, ethos, or *mentalité*, which remain basically unaltered. Here, culture is understood as an essence. By contrast, in a more materialist rendering of civilization which pays more attention to the problems of cultural transmission, the virtual isomorphism of culture is averted. Here, culture is viewed as a process. Vanaik continues that throughout modern Western intellectual history, there have been significant contestations of the cultural approach to the study of civilizations, an insistence that change is as basic as continuity to the cultural dimension of the civilization entity in question, and that the continuity of political structures may often better explain the continuity of the cultural tradition itself. Such an understanding wholly rejects Huntington's insistence on religion being the determining component of culture. As opposed to the idea of religious resurrection proposed by Huntington, Vanaik demonstrates how there is an increasing desirability and possibility of a decline of religion as the space occupied by it is shrinking in modern societies. He admits that humans must have identity for psychological wellbeing and stability, however this need for identity now exists more for personal-social, rather than for cosmic-meaning reasons. Therefore, religious identity, *per se*, is neither inescapable, nor essential.[56]

Ethical Critique

The ethical critique condemns the immoral implications of Huntington's thesis.

---

[54] Vanaik, Achin 1997 *The Furies of Indian Communalism: Religion, Modernity and Secularization,* Verso, pp 130-137.
[55] Achin Vanaik endorses Raymond Williams' dynamic vision of culture as a process rather than a static view of culture as a 'class of things, shared' or a 'state of affairs' because the former is more fit for modern societies. For details see Williams, Raymond 1981 *Culture,* Fontana Press.
[56] Vanaik, op.cit, pp 65-129.

It proclaims that the clash of civilizations is a purposeful thesis that serves particular interests. Edward W. Said revealed that Huntington formulated his thesis while keeping an eye on rivals in the policy making ranks, theorists such as Francis Fukuyama and his 'end of history' idea, as well as the legions who had celebrated the onset of globalism and the dissipation of the states. Naz Wasim confirms that Huntington's thesis was a strategy to influence US foreign and defence policy.[57] In this regard, Hans Kung pinpoints the fact that Huntington was an advisor to the Pentagon in 1994.

Interestingly the personal ambition of Huntington was in tandem with the expansionary goals of US policy makers. The declaration of a possibility of World War III by Huntington fit well with the needs of the US arms industry. Noam Chomsky highlights that every year the White House presents to Congress a statement describing reasons for having a huge military budget. For fifty years, it used the pretext of a Soviet threat. However, after the end of the Cold War, that pretext was gone. Therefore, Huntington constructed the Islamic threat as a pretext to justify the need for maintaining and enhancing the defence-industrial base.[58] Thus, Huntington's thesis is in fact an *enemy discourse* that looks for new enemies. Muhammad Asadi further adds that Huntington's thesis serves two purposes. First, it enables the extraction of manpower and funds from the American people for the ulterior motives of American elites. Second, it alters the agenda of the rest of the world, particularly the underdeveloped part of it, away from domestic issues, and towards conducting America's wars.[59]

The ethical critique also asserts that Huntington's thesis is a self-fulfilling prophecy. It causes the expected event to occur, and thus, verifies its own accuracy. John Ikenberry says that Huntington's thesis is the civilizational equivalent of the security dilemma, in which misperception about the other eventually increases tension, and then leads to conflict. He feels that if the ideas of prominent thinkers have any impact on the real world, then the clash of civilizations thesis is potentially dangerous.[60] Amartya Sen, in a letter to Robert Kagan, expressed similar apprehension by stating that the violent tendency within Islam is not only because of the 'pull' of resurgent Islam, but also due to the 'push' of distancing coming from the Western parochialism that characterises Huntington's thesis.[61]

---

[57] Wasim, Naz 'Challenging Samuel Huntington's The Clash of Civilizations: The Shared Tradition of Europe, and Islam' in International Conference on the Dialogue of Civilizations, 31 July to 3 August, 2001 available at http://www.unu.edu/dialogue/conf-report.pdf

[58] http://www.india-seminar.com/2002/509/509%20noam%20chomsky.htm

[59] Asadi, op.cit.

[60] Ikenberry, op.cit, pp 162-163

[61] Amartya Sen, letter to Robert Kagan, 'Is there a Clash of Civilizations?', *Slate*

The validity of all these criticisms was proved to a considerable extent by several empirical studies. Pippa Norris and Ronald Inglehart used the World Values Survey database to compare the social and political values of Western and Muslim societies and concluded that Muslims have no less democratic ideals than the West.[62] Manus I. Mildarsky similarly found that there was no negative association between Islam and democracy.[63] Bruce Russet, John Oneal, and Michaelene Cox investigated inter-state disputes between 1885 to 1994 to conclude that it is not the civilizations, but the traditional realist and liberal variables – geography, power alliances, democracy, economic interdependence, and international organisation – that define the fault lines along which international conflict is apt to occur.[64]

Though the critiques of Huntington's thesis point out its various flaws, they are much weaker when it comes to explaining its receptivity. This is not just amongst decision-makers and shapers, but also amongst the general population. It is to this point that the discipline of psychology can provide a critical insight.

Designing a Psychological Critique

Despite the copious criticisms targeting Huntington's epistemology, methodology and ethics – the clash of civilizations thesis flourishes throughout the globe. Any attempt to check this trend requires a serious probing into the issue of how people become so receptive to such a provocative body of knowledge. In other words, how does a provocative idea, like Huntington's thesis, interact with the psyche of the people, so as to transform them into its agents?

In this regard, Philip G. Zimbardo notes that the process by which hostile schemas, aggressive scripts and other types of knowledge structures are activated is a cognitive one that can – with practice – become completely automatic and operate without awareness.[65] As such, the easy receptivity of Huntington's thesis can be grasped by decoding its cognitive role. A more

Magazine, (Posted Friday, May 5, 2006, at 11:52 PM).

[62] Norris, op.cit, pp 11-12.

[63] Mildarsky, Manus I. 1998 'Democracy and Islam: Implication for Civilization Conflict and the Democratic Peace', *International Studies Quarterly*, Vol. 42, No. 3, pp. 485-511.

[64] Russet, Bruce (et.al) September 2002 'Clash of Civilizations or Realism and Liberalism Deja Vu? Some Evidence', *Journal of Peace Research*, Vol. 378, No. 5, pp 583-608.

[65] Zimbardo, Philip G. 2004 'A Situationist Perspective on the Psychology of Evil' in Miller, Arthur G.(ed.) *The Social Psychology of Good and Evil,* Guilford Publications, pp 178-182.

detailed account of the psychic dimension of knowledge structures can be traced in the work of Ilan Gur Zeev. He claims that the control of the legitimisation, production, representation, and distribution of knowledge makes possible the reduction of human beings into 'subjects', who then function as the agents of that knowledge structure. He refers to such a control as 'normalised education' and explains that this normalised education commands the psyche of the subjects on four levels: (1) Control of the psychic constitution and strivings of the subjects; (2) Control of the conceptual apparatus and its integration with the psychic level of the subjects; (3) Control of the collective and private self-consciousness of the subjects; (4) Control of the functions of the subjects in order to minimise the possibilities for change in the representation of reality that normalised education reflects and serves.[66] These insights support the inference that Huntington's thesis acquires receptivity by controlling the psyche of the people in a way that any normalised education does.

Keith Lehrer further elaborates upon the psychological functioning of an accepted knowledge structure. He states that the acceptance of knowledge is a sort of mental state that has a specific functional role, in thought, inference, and action.[67] He claims that when a person accepts a body of knowledge, then the person will apply it in the appropriate circumstances and use it to justify other conclusions. Such a person will reason and act in a certain manner assuming the truth of that body of knowledge. In this regard, Huntington's thesis can be viewed as an accepted body of knowledge that thrives upon its ability to mould the reasoning and actions of people in a restrictive manner.

The academic discipline of psychology can serve as a lens through which the nature and warrants of Huntington's thesis can be seen, and its subterfuges and destructive forces can be perceived. Psychology broadly offers three models for studying human behaviour –*psychoanalytic, behaviouristic* and *humanistic-existential.* Each of these models can be utilised for evaluating the receptivity of Huntington's thesis. Since each model is rooted in a distinct philosophical tradition and relies on a distinct methodology, they provide a distinct understanding of the psychological mediation involved in the translation of the aggressive claims of Huntington's thesis into violent outcomes. However, this study holds the opinion that the humanistic-existential model is more appropriate as it has a methodological edge over the other models.

---

[66] Michael A. Peters. 2015 *Education, Globalization and the State in the Age of Terrorism,* Routledge, p. 233.

[67] Lehrer, Keith 2000 *Theory of Knowledge,* Westview Press, pp 39-40.

Psychoanalytic Model

The first use of the term 'psychoanalysis' was made by Freud in 1896 in his paper entitled *Heredity and the Aetiology of the Neurosis.*[68] The basic tenet was a deterministic theory of human behaviour based on the laws of the mind. For Freud, psychoanalysis was aimed at discovering the functioning of the unconscious. His functionalist approach was two-fold: one level was concerned with inherent instincts and the other level was concerned with the psychic mechanism of displacement.[69] First, it proposed that there is an inherent instinct in human beings that is destructive and moves towards self-destruction. Freud described it as the opposite to the principle of Eros, and called it Thanos – the death wish. Second, it is proposed that individuals displace emotions, frustration and aggression – which are essentially part of their private emotional lives – away from their personal relationships and project them into political life. The themes of sex and aggression are interlinked in Freudian literature.[70]

Freud assigned a specific role to civilization and religion under his twofold approach. Firstly, since instinctual aggression is a hard reality of life, which the civilised society finds a bitter pill to swallow – religion is discovered as the *future of an illusion.* Religion promises happiness after death as a compensation for the renunciation of instinctual aggression in this life.[71] Carl Jung concludes that instead of a blissful feeling of merger with a literal God (conventionally a religious experience), religion can be an inward connection to one's psyche.[72] Secondly, since there is a psychic mechanism of aggression displacement at work, the institutionalised civilization or religion binds together a considerable number of people in love so long as there are people of other civilizations or religions who receive the manifestation of their aggressiveness. Rene Girard claims that religion offers a fantasy system to enact immensely violent acts in a sacrosanct manner to preserve order in society.[73]

---

[68] Singh, Amar Kumar December 1998 'The Concept of Man in Psychology', *Social Change,* Vol.28, No.4, p. 6.
[69] Bloom, William 1990 *Personal Identity, National Identity and International Relations,* Cambridge, pp 7-8.
[70] Freud, Sigmund 1953 *Civilization and its Discontents,* Hogarth Press, p 85. (originally published in 1930).
[71] Freud, Sigmund 1961 *Future of an Illusion,* Hogarth Press (originally published in 1927).
[72] Piven, Jerry S. 2002 'On the Psychosis (Religion) of Terrorists' in Stout, Chris E. (ed) *The Psychology of Terrorism* Vol. III, Praeger , pp 119-140.
[73] Stirling, Mack, C. 'Violent Religion: Rene Girard's Theory of Culture' in Ellens, op.cit, pp11-50.

This psychoanalytic understanding of civilization can help to comprehend the basic appeal of Huntington's thesis. Huntington's categorisation of the global population along so-called civilizational lines mainly focuses on religious divisions. Since people are, by and large, religious and they experience 'religion' and 'violence' as yoked together, they find the idea of civilizational clash somewhat attractive and normal.

However, the psychoanalytic model becomes problematic as it is not compatible with certain assertions of Huntington's thesis. For instance, the psychoanalytic image of religion as an 'illusion' or 'fantasy system' is universal in terms of applicability. Thus, Huntington's act of singling out Islam as the most perverse form of religion that particularly breeds demons is objectionable. The motivation for religiously driven murderous zeal can be traced in radical extremists, not only among Muslims, but certainly among Christians and Jews, as well. Moreover, since the inherently aggressive instinct is universal, there may be a considerable number of people who do not believe in religion but are violent. Furthermore, there may be people who do not consciously or unconsciously practice religion for the purpose of suppressing or releasing their violent instincts.

The psychoanalytic model became obsolete as its traditional method of introspection was opposed by the movement of positivism, objectivism and empiricism that became a zeitgeist by the end of the nineteenth century. The early twentieth century saw the rise of behaviourism which stood for the use of the experimental method of the natural sciences.

Behaviouristic Model

This model was born in 1913 with a paper written by J.B. Watson entitled *Psychology as the Behaviourist Views It.* The basic maxim was the positive correlation between stimulus and response. Conclusions derived from animal experiments were applied to study human behaviour. The first classic experiment was carried out by Ivan Pavlov, wherein a dog was repeatedly presented with food and sound simultaneously. Consequently, the sound acquired the strength of food and created saliva in a dog's mouth even in the absence of food. The dog had developed a *conditioned reflex*.[74] In 1914 Pavlov discovered that a neurosis-like symptom can be developed in dogs by disturbing the conditioned reflex. In an experiment a dog was conditioned to discriminate between a circle and an ellipse. The ellipse was then gradually modified to look more and more like a circle. The dog failed to discriminate

---

[74] Pavlov, Ivan 1941 ' Lectures on Conditioned Reflexes', Vol. 2: *Conditioned Reflexes and Psychiatry* translated and edited by W.H. Gantt, Lawrence and Wishart Ltd. available at http://www.heretical.com/pavlov/chap-50.html

and showed great discomfort and tension. It tore off the experimental apparatus and exhibited signs of nervous breakdown or 'experimental neurosis'.

In the light of the conclusions derived from Pavlov's experiments, Huntington's thesis can be viewed as a stimulus that provokes violent response in both Muslim and Western societies. Within Muslim society it works in two ways. Firstly, it functions as a conditioning mechanism that repeatedly demonises Muslims, thereby psychologically compelling them to act as such. Secondly, it works as an irritant that disturbs the traditionally conditioned reflexes of Muslims by insulting them for how they have always been. The discrimination between the Islamic notion of 'good' and 'bad', as it traditionally occurs to Muslim minds, is deeply distorted by Huntington's thesis, which in turn fuels violent tendencies.

If Huntington's thesis presents an inferior picture of Islam, it projects a superior image of the West, thereby stimulating an aggressive response from the West to assert and safeguard its abnormally elevated pride. The net result of this deliberate construction of a gulf between the respective self-esteem of Islam and the West is a sort of academic warfare which can be witnessed by the development of a counter-thesis in response to the clash of civilizations thesis of Huntington. Gilles Kepel in his book *The War for Muslim Minds* portrays Ayman al-Zawahiri's text *Knights Under the Prophet's Banner* as a jihadist reading of the clash of civilizations. Michael Dunn refers to the popularity of these texts in the Muslim world and reveals that these texts are developed as an essential form of discourse by two powerful groups of elites – the Western policymakers and the leaders of the al-Qaida network – in order to infuriate the masses.

The behaviouristic model was further enriched when Pavlov's experiments found an extension in the work of B.F. Skinner, J.B. Watson and E.L. Thordike. They conducted learning experiments where response occurred without a visible stimulus – similar to what often happens in real life situations. For instance, Skinner placed a food-deprived rat in a box, which then accidently pressed a lever that released a food pellet. The rat in Skinner's experiment had to operate upon the environment, unlike the dog in Pavlov's experiment which did nothing to obtain the food. These learning experiments emphasised the role of environment and started a trend which shifted the biological orientation of psychology to a socio-cultural one. Neo-Freudians like Adler, Horney, Fromm and Marcuse argued in a Marxist vein that the demand for repression of instincts comes from the alienating socio-economic structure of a society, unlike the Freudian understanding where repression is a protective ego-defence created by the individual.[75]

This neo-Freudian/Marxist line of argument suggests that the notion of civilizational clash wins acceptance because it reflects the aspirations of rich people in the West and the destitute people of the Muslim world, who find themselves at war with each other due to their location within a particular socio-cultural circumstance. As such, the acceptability of the idea of civilizational clash should be perceived as a symptom of socio-economic deprivations faced by Muslims in the context of global capitalist insecurity.

However, the behaviouristic model also becomes disputable as it fails to adequately deal with certain aspects of Huntington's thesis. In addition, there are exceptions among elites, as well as masses, that neither believe in, nor respond to, the provocative stimulus unleashed by Huntington's thesis. Moreover, a similar socio-cultural circumstance does not always ensure behavioural similarity. Responses to the same objective situation differ considerably from person to person, depending on each person's social learning history (i.e. personality) and present state of mind (i.e. which knowledge structure is currently most accessible).[76] Therefore every rich American and every poor Muslim need not find a foe in each other.

The extremely restrictive explanation of human behaviour as a response to stimulus increasingly became unacceptable. Since behaviour will always be conditioned, it is only wise to condition it efficiently. But, shocked and appalled critics – sensing faint hints of fascism – wondered who will decide the goals of humanity? Who is to be trusted to carry out the proper conditioning? These worries paved the way for the humanistic–existential model of psychology that rejected both the savage image of man nourished by psychoanalysis as well as the robot image of man nurtured by behaviourism. It thereby attempted to find a middle ground between these two extreme positions.

Humanistic-Existential Model

This model focused on the uniqueness of human existence and provided maximum scope for human agency. It attempted to understand human needs as they stem from the conditions of existence.[77] However, this did not imply a total surrender to conditioning factors as an explanation of human behaviour. The emphasis on experience, stress on creativity, concern for dignity and

---

[75]   Singh, p.19.

[76]   Zimbardo, p.177.

[77]   Fromm, Eric 1955, *The Sane Society*, Fawcett Premier Books, pp 31-32.

allegiance to meaningful problems for study constituted its foundation stones.[78] It realised that the beautifully executed, precise, and elegant experiments of psychology, in at least half the cases, have nothing to do with enduring human problems.[79] Maslow lamented that psychology has been long obsessed with the deviant, the sick and the criminal, ignoring the normal. Laing further argued that the abnormal is indeed a sane person maladjusted in an insane society.[80] Thus, from the standpoint of human values, the abnormal is less crippled than the kind of normal person who has lost individuality in the process of adjustment in society.[81] Szasz asserted that the myth of mental illness is created by the society.[82] The standard psychiatric patient is an artefact of a standard psychiatrist and a standard mental hospital. In fact, human behaviour is exquisitely rational moving with subtle and ordered complexity towards the goals our organism is endeavouring to achieve.[83]

According to this model, a combination of two paradoxical forces determine human behaviour. The first is the free agency of the individual who is personally responsible for creating meaning in a seemingly meaningless world. The second is the compulsion of the conditions of existence that affects the individual's willingness or unwillingness to create or believe in a particular set of meanings. From this perspective, Huntington's thesis becomes agreeable because of two reasons. The first is Huntington's willingness to generate a specific notion of reality and the second is the people's choice to identify their own perception of reality with that notion. In other words, Huntington's presentation of an imagined reality (i.e. false consciousness), which is fraught with a civilizational clash, becomes an actual reality (i.e. false real consciousness) only when people choose to internalise it and act, or react, upon it.[84] The purpose behind Huntington's choice to present reality in a particular way and the people's choice to accept it lies in their respective conditions of existence. In the given circumstance, the prospect of a civilizational clash serves the purpose of its believers,

---

[78] Buhler, C. and Allen M. 1972 *Introduction to Humanistic Psychology*, Brooks / Cole, pp1-2.
[79] Maslow, A. 'A Philosophy of Psychology' in Severin, F. (ed) 1965 *Humanistic Viewpoints in Psychology,* McGraw Hill, pp 17-33.
[80] Laing, Ronald D. 1967 *The Politics of Experience,* Ballantine, p. 58.
[81] Fromm, Eric P 1942 *Fear of Freedom,* Routledge, p 120.
[82] Szasz, T.S. 1960 'The Myth of Mental Illness' *American Psychologist*, Vol. 15, pp 113-118.
[83] Rogers, C.R. 1961 *On Becoming a Person*, Houghton Mifflin, p 194.
[84] Achin Vanaik uses the term 'false real consciousness' to suggest that any ideology that arouses 'false consciousness' does not posit a false world as an alternative to the real world, but a false way of experiencing and relating to the real world. See Vanaik, p.79.

thereby enabling it to acquire a meaning even if it is utterly meaningless.

The discernments obtained from the humanistic-existential model forcefully challenge the authenticity of Huntington's thesis. They reveal the disguised manipulative venture of Huntington who disregards the uniqueness of human existence by deliberately laying down the standards of a 'truly civilised society' and demonising those who fail to fit those standards, thereby manufacturing a myth of civilizational pathology.

Under the conditions of the post-Cold War world, the superficial concept of 'bloody Islamic borders' enabled Huntington to gain an influential position among US foreign policymakers who were desperately looking for an alarming sermon which could cover their aggressive policies under the mask of legitimate defensive action. Huntington's intentional ignorance of the painful conditions of existence in Muslim societies and his attribution of their consequent frustration to a kind of civilizational-cultural-religious disorder gave a new meaning to persisting political issues. This new meaning served the purpose of its believers at many levels. Firstly, it helped US policymakers to divert the attention of both Muslims and non-Muslims away from the genuine suffering and the creative potential of the Islamic world, thereby facilitating an ensured American hegemony. Secondly, it allowed the fanatics in both Islamic and Western societies to enrage the masses, thereby paving the way for satisfying their personal ambitions.

Though Huntington's dangerous motive becomes quite apparent as soon as he activates his abstract idea of 'civilizational identity' by awakening a hatred for other civilizations, it is well-received by the people who find it relevant and useful in their living conditions.[85] The cascading effect of the abstract idea of 'civilizational identity' totally obscures the complexity of human identity formation and thus weakens the effort at human emancipation. However, the humanistic-existential model is optimistic in its assertion that Huntington's thesis acquires receptivity, not because it discloses some identifiable ultimate truth about innate human nature or emits provocative stimulations to which human beings are bound to succumb. The popularity of it is largely an outcome of the personal choice of human beings who are embedded in their respective conditions of existence as free agents.

As such, the issue of acceptance or rejection becomes a matter of free choice and the onus for exploring its harmful implications rest on free individuals.

---

[85] Huntington subscribes to Michael Dibdin's idea, as expressed in his novel *'Dead Lagoon',* that unless we hate what we are not, we cannot love what we are. See Huntington, Samuel P. 1996 *The Clash of Civilizations and the Remaking of World Order*, Penguin, p.20

The essence of this insight can be traced in the following Zimbardo homily: While a few bad apples might spoil the barrel (filled with good fruit/people), a barrel filled with vinegar will always transform sweet cucumbers into sour pickles – regardless of the best intentions, resilience and genetic nature of those cucumbers. So, does it make more sense to spend our resources on an attempt to identify, isolate and destroy the few bad apples or to learn how vinegar works so that we can teach cucumbers how to avoid undesirable vinegar barrels? The next chapter attempts to demonstrate the 'vinegar-effect' of Huntington's thesis in the context of post-9/11 Afghanistan.

3

Huntington Amongst the Afghans: Revisiting the Clash of Civilizations Thesis After 9/11

The spectre of a clash of civilizations between Islam and the West has frequently loomed after 9/11 and the subsequent US-led war on terrorism in Afghanistan. Ziauddin Sardar and Merryl Wyn Davies asked:

> is it surprising that many in the West see today's war on terrorism as the prelude to a renewed clash of civilizations? The question is in every newspaper and magazine. It did not need the right-wing American political scientist Huntington to pose the question – the idea has never actually gone away.[86]

William Kristol and Robert Kagan declared that post-9/11 Afghanistan was going to resemble the clash of civilizations everyone had hoped to avoid.[87] This view gained strength when the perpetrators themselves presented the 9/11 attacks as 'jihad', or Islamic holy war, against Christians and Jews,[88] and the then US President George W. Bush reiterated the same spirit by using the

---

[86] Sardar, Ziauddin and Davies, Merryl Wyn 2004 *American Dream, Global Nightmare,* Cambridge, pp. 53-54.

[87] Kristol, William and Kagan, Robert October 29, 2001 'The Gathering Storm', *The Weekly Standard*, pp. 13-14.

[88] Commins, David 'Osama bin Laden's Declaration of Jihad Against Americans', *Milestone Documents in World History: Exploring the Primary Sources that Shaped the World*, available at http://salempress.com/store/pdfs/bin_Laden.pdf ; Wedgwood, Ruth 2002 'Al Qaeda, Terrorism and Military Commissions', *American Journal of International Law,* Vol. 96, No. 2, pp. 328-337.

word 'crusade' with its connotations of a Christian holy war against Muslims.[89] The war in Afghanistan still continues. After the completion of Operation Neptune Spear in 2011, which caused the demise of al-Qaida leader Osama bin Laden, US President Barack Obama announced that his country would never be at war with Islam.[90] Despite this, outraged Islamic organisations like Jamaat-e-Islami and Jamaat-ud-Dawah declared Osama bin Laden as a 'Martyr of Islam' and called upon Muslims to rise up against the US.

The portrayal of post-9/11 Afghanistan as a venue for a clash of civilizations should not be based on casual political rhetoric, but on serious historical analysis. This chapter aims to reveal the specific historical factors that refute the applicability of Huntington's thesis to 9/11 and the subsequent US-led war on terrorism in Afghanistan. However, the theoretical inapplicability of Huntington's thesis does not automatically imply the absence of Huntington's popularity in Afghanistan. How do Huntington's ideas win psychological receptivity amongst the Afghans and what implications does it have on their political lives? The chapter goes further to examine the general history of 'political reception' in Afghan politics, thereby facilitating an assessment of the impact of Huntington's ideas on the politics of post-9/11 Afghanistan. The chapter is divided into three sections. The first section provides a historical background to 9/11. The second section highlights the anti-Huntingtonian nature of 9/11 and its aftermath. The third section uncovers the psychological mechanism that grants political receptivity to Huntington's ideas in Afghanistan, thereby exposing its harmful impact on post-9/11 Afghan politics.

Historical Background of 9/11

Commenting on the violent history of Afghanistan, Martin Ewans wrote:

> If there has been an overriding feature of their history, it is that it has been a history of conflict – of invasion, battles and sieges, of vendettas, assassinations and massacres, of tribal feuding, dynastic strife and civil war. Rarely have the Afghans allowed themselves, or have allowed others with whom they have come into contact, to lead out their lives in peace.[91]

While ethnic conflicts have largely shaped their domestic disputes, the

---

[89]   Acharya, Amitav 'Clash of Civilizations? No, of National Interests and Principles' available at http://www.cpdsindia.org/clashofcivilizations.htm

[90]   Obama, Barack 2007 'Remarks in Washington, DC: The War We Need to Win', *The American Presidency Project* available at http://www.presidency.ucsb.edu/ws/?pid=77040

[91]   Ewans, Martin 2001 *Afghanistan: A New History,* Curzon Press, p.9.

interference of foreign powers has often elevated the status of domestic ethnic conflicts to actual, or potential, international wars. The 9/11 attacks that triggered the global war on terrorism can be understood in the light of this historical trend.

The snow-covered mountains, barren deserts and rolling steppes of Afghanistan accommodates approximately 30 million people who are divided into more than twenty ethnic groups. Of these ethnic groups, the prominent ones are Pashtuns, Tajiks, Uzbeks, Hazaras and Nuristanis. These groups tell distinct stories about their historical origins, reside in distinct regions, speak distinct languages and practice distinct professions. The unequal power relations between these groups has historically acted as a source of conflict. In fact, none of the ethnic groups share the dominant position – and disposition – of their Pashtun compatriots. Pashtuns, who account for approximately 42 percent of the country's population, have their own code of conduct called 'Pashtunwali' which includes obligations not only of hospitality and honour, but also of revenge. Disputes over the questions of honour and revenge have been endemic features of Pashtun life. Tajiks, Uzbeks, Hazaras and Nuristanis have only barely or begrudgingly accepted control from a central administration in Kabul, dominated by the Pashtuns, and this link has been exposed throughout Afghanistan's history with various internal conflicts, uprisings, and inter-ethnic clashes.[92]

In addition to ethnic cleavages, there is a religious divide between the Shia Hazara population and the predominant Sunni population of the rest of Afghanistan. If Hazaras constitute a minority group on religious grounds, the more alienated are the Nuristanis who were known as 'kafirs', or infidels, before being converted to Islam. Tajiks, Uzbeks, Hazaras, and Nuristanis typically consider Pashtuns as oppressors.[93] However, they are not united in their struggle against Pashtuns and share mutually conflictive relations. Even within ethnic and religious boundaries, the regional divides are crucial in germinating conflicts. The enmities and bitter struggles amongst the people of Afghanistan spring from tribal, sub-tribal, and regional differences which escape definition in terms of modern political theories.[94]

Despite the bonds of Islam, which was introduced in Afghanistan as early as 652 A.D., the sense of national unity has always been weak and the state has

---

[92] Clements, Frank A. 2003 *Conflict in Afghanistan: An Encyclopaedia*, ABC-CLIO, p. xiv.

[93] Glatzer, Bernt 1999 'Is Afghanistan on the Brink of Ethnic and Tribal Disintegration? in Maley, William (ed.) *Fundamentalism Reborn? Afghanistan and the Taliban*, Hurst and Company, pp. 167-181.

[94] Anwar, Raja 1998 *The Tragedy of Afghanistan*, Verso, pp 126-127.

never been strong enough to exercise effective control over the country which is fragmented along ethnic lines. While Islamic tribunals have proved useful in resolving inter-ethnic disputes pertaining to petty theft and other divisions of booty, they have not been instrumental in bringing an end to the struggle for dominance amongst the gangs, or the tribal wrangles which constitute a tradition that antedates Islam.[95]

Commenting on the ineffectiveness of Islam in producing national unity, Gilbret Achcar wrote:

> Islam has not been perceived in the twentieth century as the ideological cement of an outmoded feudal or semi-feudal class structure in Muslim societies. It has been seen instead as a basic element of national identity jeered at by the foreign Christian (or even atheist) oppressor.[96]

The Islamic element in Afghan national identity has been pointed out not just by foreign oppressors, but also by the oppressed Afghans themselves. Fred Halliday opined:

> The very condition of being oppressed…is likely to produce its own distorted forms of perception…Nationalism has illustrated this often enough…Myths of nationalism is a part of struggle, employed by both those who wish to remain in power and those who aspire to attain power.[97]

The Islamic underpinning of Afghan nationalism has been historically evoked less for fostering unity amongst the various ethnic groups, than for mobilising them against foreign intruders. One can witness a comparative togetherness amongst the Afghans when the country is threatened by a foreign enemy. The determination to remain free from foreign domination is a part of Afghan tradition.[98] But, at the same time, foreign attempts to acquire influence in world politics by manipulating the internal affairs of the country are a part of Afghan history. The 'Great Game'[99] between the Soviet Union and the US during Cold War can be viewed as a classic example of this trend. The Soviet-backed Saur Revolt in Afghanistan in 1978 established a new pattern

---

[95] Achcar, Gilbert 2004 *Eastern Cauldron,* Monthly Review Press, p. 95.

[96] Ibid, p. 49.

[97] Halliday, Fred 1996 *Islam and the Myth of Confrontation,* I. B. Tauris, pp. 5-6.

[98] Maaroof, Mohammad Khalid 1987 *Afghanistan in World Politics*, Gian Publishing House, p.6.

[99] See Griffith, John C. 1981 *Afghanistan: Key to A Continent*, Westview Press, pp. 30-55.

that was to dominate Afghan politics for the next decade and a half – a pattern of dependence on the Soviet Union.[100] The Soviet-influenced Afghan Communist Party, known as People's Democratic Party of Afghanistan (PDPA), seized power and Babrak Karmal was established as the head. The newly established Karmal regime became an irritant for both the Afghans and the Americans. The Afghans who were intolerant of foreign interference viewed Karmal as a Soviet puppet and stooge. They began to organise themselves against Karmal and initiated what became popularly known as the 'Mujahideen movement'. The Mujahideen, overwhelmingly composed of Afghans with diverse ethnic backgrounds, were split between Shia and Sunni groups, Islamic radicals, and moderates. The only unifying factor was their opposition to the regime of Karmal and the Soviet presence.[101]

To tackle the Mujahideen threat, the Soviets replaced Karmal with Najibullah, a Pashtun, in 1986.[102] But before the situation could be pacified, American aid began to reach the Mujahideen as the struggle became embroiled in Cold War politics. In order to counter the Soviet influence in Afghanistan, the US supplied stinger missiles to Mujahideen forces and trained them so that they could defeat Soviet airpower and helicopter gunships.[103] The Soviets began to realise that they were involved in a war that they could not win. In 1987, the Soviet-backed Najibullah government tried to negotiate a ceasefire but the US-backed Mujahideen refused to negotiate. The Soviet troops departed from Afghanistan on 15 February 1989 – leaving the Najibullah government to its own devices. Najibullah was forced to resign in 1992, and an 'Islamic' state of Afghanistan was established by the Mujahideen coalition government comprised of seven Sunni groups based in Pakistan. It included supporters of Karmal, Tajiks under Rabbani backed by Massoud, Uzbeks under Dostum and the Islamic faction of Nadari. It excluded Gulbuddin Hikmatyar, a Pashtun, who was an agent of Pakistan and who had unsuccessfully bombarded Rabbani's regime during the 1992-95 period.[104]

However, the unity amongst Afghans under the aegis of the Mujahideen proved to be short lived. The Mujahideen, which emerged as a response to the conflict between foreign forces, began to crumble with the withdrawal of those foreign forces from Afghanistan. By the mid-1990s, when the Cold War

---

[100]   Magnus, Ralph H. and Naby, Eden 2000 *Afghanistan: Mullah, Marx and Mujahid*, Westview Press, p.127.

[101]   Griffin, Michael 2001 *Reaping the Whirlwind: The Taliban Movement in Afghanistan*, Pluto Press, pp. 133-140.

[102]   Cordovez, D. and Harrison S. S. 1995 *Out of Afghanistan: The Inside Story of the Soviet Withdrawal*, Oxford University Press, p.140.

[103]   Urban, Mark 1990 *War in Afghanistan,* Palgrave Macmillan.

[104]   See Saikal, Amin 1999 'The Rabbani Government, 1992-1996' in Maley, William, op.cit, pp. 29-42.

had come to an end and consequently the US support for the Mujahideen was declining, the legitimacy of the Mujahideen coalition government became eroded by internal fragmentation along ethno-linguistic, tribal, sectarian and personality lines.[105] The net result was a civil war and Afghanistan was once again transformed into a state of chaos and anarchy. Meanwhile Russia and the US appeared content to see the internecine ethnic rivalry continue, as they feared that a stable Islamic Afghanistan could damage their interests in the Central and South Asian regions.

Amid the chaos generated by the civil war, Afghanistan saw the rise of the Taliban movement. It emerged in 1994 in Kandahar province. In the Taliban movement, Pashtuns of Kandahar were joined by a few Mujahideen leaders like Mullah Mohammad Omar, commanders from other Pashtun parties, Khalq PDPA members and students from madrasas that had sprung up along the Afghanistan-Pakistan border following the 1978 Soviet intervention in Afghanistan. These madrasas were run by Sunni Muslims of the Deobandi sect. The Deobandi madrasas proved popular since they combined the traditional tenets of Islam with the strict Pashtunwali code which was practiced by most Pashtuns in both Afghanistan and Pakistan.[106] The Pashtun-dominated Taliban attempted to restore peace by disarming civilians and implementing Sharia law – thereby demonstrating a strong tendency towards theocracy. They recruited foreign fighters from Arab countries, Chechnya and Pakistan – many of whom were also part of al-Qaida,[107] the organisation that was to be held responsible for the 9/11 attacks. They were influenced by the Pakistani movement called 'Jamait-i-Ulama-i-Islam' which followed the rules of the Hanaafi Sunni branch and disseminated anti-Shiite feelings. They were also inspired by Wahhabism, which emanated from Saudi Arabia.

The Taliban reflected a transnational outlook not only in terms of its membership composition and ideational inspiration, but also in terms of political ambition. Although the Taliban's immediate concern in 1996 was the consolidation of power in Afghanistan, the regime, led by Mullah Mohammad Omar, also began to extensively support militant Islamic groups around the world.[108] Besides providing a base for al-Qaida and its leader Osama bin

[105] Roy, Olivier October, 1989 'Afghanistan Back to Tribalism or on to Lebanon?', *Third World Quarterly*, Vol. 11, No.4, pp. 70-82; Saikal, Amin and Maley, William 1991 *Regime Change in Afghanistan: Foreign Intervention and the Politics of Legitimacy*, Westview Press, pp. 118-134.
[106] Rashid, Ahmed 2001 'Afghanistan: Ending the Policy Quagmire', *Journal of International Affairs,* Vol.54, No.2, p.398.
[107] Rashid, Ahmed November/December, 1999 'Taliban: Exporting Extremism', *Foreign Affairs*, Vol.78, No. 6, pp. 22-35.
[108] Lansford, Tom and Covarrubias, Jack 2003 'Osama bin Laden, Radical Islam and

Laden, the Taliban offered both overt and tacit support to a variety of terrorist organisations involved in Tajikistan, Uzbekistan, China, Bangladesh, Kashmir, Pakistan, Saudi Arabia, and the Philippines. The goal was to bring back honour, not only to Afghans, but also to the larger Pan-Islamic society which was considered to have been humiliated by Western nations led by the US.[109] Since the West was held responsible for many of the ills that had befallen Muslim society and for the failure of Muslim culture to live by the rules set out in the Quran, the revenge on the West and the indoctrination of Sharia in all cultures were viewed as a means to rectify all wrongs. Osama bin Laden issued several 'fatwas', or Islamic rulings, calling for all Muslims to kill Americans and their allies, civilian and military, as an individual duty. The International Islamic Front for Jihad against Jews and Crusaders, which Osama bin Laden had set up in Afghanistan in 1998, began to serve as a 'clearing house' and coordinating body for many terrorist groups worldwide.[110]

By 1997, the Taliban controlled about 90 percent of the country with the anti-Taliban force of Ahmad Shah Massoud holding only a small area in the Panjsheer valley.[111] Later on, Massoud was assassinated by Arabs who were thought to be associated with al-Qaida. This event compelled Saudi Arabia, the UAE and Pakistan – the only three out of the total 53 Muslim states that recognised the Taliban – to withdraw their recognition of the Taliban regime which was already under severe international condemnation on grounds of human rights abuses, destruction of pre-Islamic heritage[112] and involvement in the international drug trade. Despite the diminishing support from the international community, the Taliban and al-Qaida continued to claim open responsibility for terrorist acts in the 1990s and 2000s, 9/11 being one of them. 9/11 ironically demonstrated how the world's only superpower was not immune from the dangers and fragility of the current international system. As a reaction against 9/11, the US declared a global war on terrorism with the objective of overthrowing the Taliban, destroying al-Qaida, capturing Osama bin Laden and establishing an anti-Taliban regime in Afghanistan led by the

---

the United States' in Hayden, Patrick, Lansford, Tom and Watson, Robert P. (eds.) *America's War on Terror,* Ashgate, p.12.

[109] 'Hunting bin Laden: Who is Osama bin Laden and What Does He Want?' 1999 *PBS Frontline*, available at http://www.pbs.org/wgbh/pages/frontline/shows/binladen/who/edicts.html

[110] Alexander, Yonah and Swetnam, Michael S., p.6.

[111] Rashid, Ahmed 2001 *Taliban: Militant Islam, Oil and Fundamentalism in Central Asia*, Yale University Press.

[112] The Taliban were so fanatically pro-Islam that they destroyed many monuments of Buddha in Bamiyan province, in March, 2001, in an attempt to wipe out everything that belonged to pre-Islamic heritage. For details, see an article by Revolutionary Association of the Women of Afghanistan (RAWA) 'Shoulder to Shoulder, Hand in Hand: Resistance Under the Iron Fist in Afghanistan´, Winter 2002 *Radical History Review,* Issue 82, pp.131-140.

Northern Alliance. Some in the US foreign-policy-shaping circles viewed 9/11 as an attractive opportunity for declaring war. This opportunity was quickly seized by the US as the US-led war on terrorism was most likely to acquire global legitimacy in the wake of 9/11. After a decade of military engagement in Afghanistan, the rule of the Taliban had been replaced with a 'democratic' regime. However, the war on terrorism in Afghanistan continues.

The 9/11 attacks seemed to capture the civilizational anguish embedded in the ideological orientation and political mission of the Taliban and al-Qaida. Even the reactionary US-led global war on terrorism appeared to reinforce the theme of civilizational antagonism. However, a historical analysis of the series of events that culminated in 9/11 and shaped its aftermath suggest that any intellectual attempt to allegorise them as a clash of civilizations is misleading.

9/11 and its Aftermath: Refuting Huntington

Prior to 9/11, Afghanistan was trapped in a civil war which was essentially an 'intra-civilizational' rather than 'inter-civilizational' conflict. The rival ethnic groups of Afghanistan – chiefly Pashtun, Tajik, Uzbek, and Hazara – were trying to powerfully assert themselves over the others. Though Huntington's thesis admitted the possibility of 'intra-civilizational' conflict, it clearly ruled out the probability of its global escalation. Huntington wrote: 'Local politics is the politics of ethnicity…global politics is the politics of civilizations'.[113]

He claimed that only the violence between states and groups from different 'civilizations' carried with it the potential of global escalation, as other states and groups belonging to these 'civilizations' rally in support of their kin countries. However, his assertion proved mistaken in the context of Afghanistan as it was the domestically unchecked ambitions of ethnic Pashtuns – the majority of whom were initially organised under the Mujahideen, and later on under the Taliban and al-Qaida – coupled with the historic support that they gained not only from the Muslim world (Saudi Arabia, UAE, Pakistan, and Uzbekistan) but also from the Christian world (US and UK) that enabled them to technically develop their capabilities to such an extent that they successfully committed 9/11.

In this context, Lansford and Covarrubias argued:

> The United States, in its efforts to contain Soviet expansion,
> developed a policy habit in which Washington tended to

---

[113] Huntington, Samuel P. 1996 *The Clash of Civilizations and the Remaking of World Order,* Penguin, p.28.

abandon the client when the Soviet threat was no longer pertinent. Afghanistan was no exception to this…Once great power interest in the country ended, the different factions within the Mujahideen were left out without the leadership necessary for the transition to a broad-based national government. This allowed the Taliban [and al-Qaida] to gain ascendency.[114]

In fact, one of the factors behind the manifestation of 9/11 was the half-done strategic manipulation of an 'intra-civilizational' conflict that backfired and in turn provoked an escalated global war on terrorism, thereby questioning the theoretical propositions of Huntington.

The US and UK held al-Qaida responsible for 9/11 on the basis of the video tape released by Osama bin Laden, whereby he welcomed the attacks. His gesture was believable as he had previously called for aggressive action against the Americans through his declarations. Though the declarations made by Osama bin Laden possessed religious overtones, they indicated that his basic grievance was not religious/cultural/civilizational, but 'political'. His sense of historic injustice towards Muslim society did not emanate from the unfair religious maxims of Christianity or Judaism in general, but from the unjust foreign policies of the US and its allies. His 'Declaration of War Against the Americans Occupying the Land of the Two Holy Places' (1996) and 'Jihad Against Jews and Crusaders' (1998) opened with the phrase 'Praise be to Allah/God', thereby emitting strong religious hints.

However, his religious provocation was motivated by the political purpose of mobilising the masses in Muslim society against the political wrongs committed by the Americans – their illegal occupation of Islamic holy lands, their unbalanced pro-Israel stance in the Israel-Palestine conflict, and their dubious policy of supporting authoritarian regimes in Lebanon, Jordan and Saudi Arabia – while claiming to promote democratic regimes in Iraq and Afghanistan.[115] He wrote:

> No one argues today about three facts that are known to everyone…First, for over seven years the United States has been occupying the lands of Islam…plundering its riches, dictating to its rulers, humiliating its people, terrorizing its neighbours…Second, despite the great devastation inflicted on the Iraqi people,…the Americans are once again trying to

---

[114] Lansford, Tom and Covarrubias, Jack, p.14.
[115] Interview with Osama bin Laden with American ABC-TV, broadcast on 10th June, 1998.

> repeat the horrific massacres…Third, if the Americans' aims behind these wars are religious and economic, the aim is also to serve the Jews' petty state… The crimes and sins committed by the Americans are a clear declaration of war on God, his messenger and Muslims.[116]

A careful reading of Osama bin Laden's statements reflects his confused stance on the 'religious' motivations behind American political moves. At one point, he sceptically wondered: '*If* the Americans' aims behind these wars are religious…,' whereas at another point he asserted: 'The crimes and sins committed by the Americans are a *clear* declaration of war on God…' Though Osama bin Laden seemed confused about the religious motivations of the Americans, he was certain about the need to take violent action against their unjust political behaviour. Utilising religion as a tool to evoke revengeful sentiments among Muslims, he appealed: 'The ulema have throughout Islamic history unanimously agreed that the jihad is the individual duty if the enemy destroys the Muslim countries.'[117]

Like Osama bin Laden, the rhetoric of 'civilizations' repeatedly crept into the language of former US President George W. Bush. While addressing a joint session of Congress and the American people on September 20, 2001, Bush outlined his vision for the war on terrorism by declaring – 'this is civilization's fight'.[118] However, while speaking to the UN General Assembly on September 21, 2004, he stated: 'There is no clash of civilizations'.[119] Though he chose to attack Afghanistan as the first of a series of attacks which he vowed to undertake as he waged a global war on terrorism, his policy was not driven by any religious motive of annexing the Muslim country, but by the political goals of hunting Osama bin Laden, crushing al-Qaida and replacing the Taliban with a pro-US regime. These declared political goals were accompanied by the hidden geo-strategic ambition of securing a long-term entry in the internal affairs of Central and South Asia. The statement made by James L. Jones, the US President's national security adviser, confirms this line of thinking. While speaking on CNN's 'State of the Union', he indicated the possibility of a long stay of US troops in Afghanistan. He said: 'We have strategic interests in South Asia that should not be measured in terms of finite times…We are going to be in the region for a long time'.[120]

Both al-Qaida and the Bush administration pretended to speak on behalf of

---

[116] Ibid.
[117] Ibid.
[118] http://www.whitehouse.gov/news/releases/2001/09/20010920-8.html
[119] http://www.whitehouse.gov/news/releases/2004/06/20040629-4.html
[120] Mazzetti, Mark December 7, 2009, *The New York Times.*

their respective 'civilizations', but none could be considered as a core representative in the absence of unanimous backing from the entire 'civilization' to which they belonged. After 9/11, al-Qaida was denounced by Saudi Arabia, Iran, Indonesia, Malaysia and Pakistan. On the night of 9/11, Iranians gathered outside the US embassy to offer their sympathy. In Malaysia, Prime Minister Mahathir bin Mohammad made it difficult for Malaysian jihadists to travel to Afghanistan to fight alongside the Taliban and al-Qaida. In Pakistan, President Pervez Musharraf criticised the terrorists for giving Islam a bad name. The Organization of the Islamic Conference condemned Osama bin Laden's terrorism, but did not condemn the US response.[121] Appalled by the terrorists' methods and the loss of so many innocent lives, most religious leaders in Islamic societies condemned the attacks as un-Islamic. A section of Muslim society not only ridiculed the attacks but also went a step further to participate in the war against the perpetrators. The US-led campaign in Afghanistan acquired significant support not only from Christians but also from Muslims living both within and outside of the country. Besides the support of anti-Taliban forces residing in Afghanistan, the US-led war on terrorism was contributed to by the military forces of Turkey, Uzbekistan and Pakistan.

While the idea of a post-9/11 war on terrorism in Afghanistan was appreciated by a fraction of Muslim society, it was severely criticised by a large section of Christians in Western Europe and America. On 29 September 2001, as many as 20,000 people demonstrated in Washington DC denouncing the impending invasion of Afghanistan.[122] Demonstrations were also held in the Netherlands, Spain and Greece. Over 10,000 people filled Amsterdam's central square for an open-air meeting with 'Justice, Not Revenge' as a slogan of the protest.[123] In Scotland, around 1,500 people gathered in Glasgow for a rally against the military action. In Australia, thousands of people demonstrated in the cities of Sydney, Melbourne, Perth and Adelaide.[124] In Germany, more than 25,000 protesters took to the streets in cities across the country. In Berlin, the largest demonstration drew 15,000 people to the central square in a rally that followed several marches throughout the city under the banner 'No War – Stand Up for Peace'.[125] On 18 November 2001, a large crowd – police

---

[121]   Samuel P. Huntington in an interview with Nathan Gardels available at http://www.digitalnpq.org/global_services/global%20viewpoint/10-22-01.html

[122]   'New York City Protest Opposes War in Afghanistan' available at http://www.wsws.org/articles/2001/oct2001/nyc-o12.shtml

[123]   Sherman, Paul 'Tens of Thousands March in the US and Europe Against War Preparations' available at http://www.wsws.org/articles/2001/oct2001/wash-o03.shtml

[124]   '20,000 Join Anti-War Protest' available at http://www.guardian.co.uk/world/2001/oct/13/afghanistan.terrorism5

[125]   Featherstone, Liza 'Operation Enduring Protest' available at http://www.thenation.com/article/operation-enduring-protest

estimated 15,000, organisers estimated 100,000 – took part in a march in London to demonstrate against the war in Afghanistan. Many protesters waved placards reading 'Stop the War' and 'Not in My Name'. Paul Marsden told the rally:

> You are sending a powerful message to Number 10 and to the White House that we are not simply going to allow the atrocities of September 11 to be replaced with further atrocities in Afghanistan.[126]

Later, some 30 million people in Western countries participated in the global anti-war rallies of 15 February 2003.[127] On 20 March 2009, thousands of Americans, some bearing mock coffins to protest war casualties, took to the streets on the sixth anniversary of the 2003 Iraq invasion to protest the wars in Iraq and Afghanistan.[128] The protests in response to the label 'axis of evil' that the US had assigned to a few Muslim states symbolised worldwide concern for the narrative of al-Qaida and demonstrated anti-American sentiment not only in the Muslim world, but also in the West.[129] The overall nature of political response to 9/11 refutes Huntington's principle of 'rallying behind' the countries of 'their kin'.

After ten years of incessant military campaigning in Afghanistan, the US-led Coalition Force still relied heavily on the cooperation of Afghan warlords to fight against the Taliban and al-Qaida, whereas the government of Afghanistan remains somewhat dependent upon the US-led Coalition Force for security, military and financial needs. The real threat to the government is posed not by Christians, but by the orthodox Muslim hardliners residing within Afghanistan and the frontiers of Pakistan.[130] Islam, as practiced in Afghanistan, has always been divided across softliners / moderates and hardliners / radicals who are associated with different religious schools that provide their own distinct interpretation of Islam/Quran – Sunni Hanaafi, Shia Jaafari, Mild Sufi Qadiriya, Orthodox Sufi Naqshbandi and the like.[131] The

---

[126] 'Thousands Join Anti-War March' available at http://news.bbc.co.uk/2/hi/uk_news/1662656.stm

[127] Alam, M. Shahid 'Is this a Clash of Civilizations?' available at http://www.mediamonitors.net/mshahidalam2.html

[128] 'As US Public Sours on Afghanistan, Obama Calls for 'Exit Strategy' available at http://www.csmonitor.com/World/terrorism-security/2009/0323/p99s01-duts.html

[129] Shibley Telhani Conference, May 14-15, 2002, 'The United States, Europe and the Muslim World: Revitalizing Relations after September 11', *CSIS: Islam Program,* Washington D.C. For European criticism, see 81st note.

[130] Peimani, Hooman 2003 *Falling Terrorism and Rising Conflict,* Prager.

[131] Hiro, Dilip 2002 *War Without End: The Rise of Islamic Terrorism and Global Response,* Routledge, pp.179-264.

fragmented picture of Islam in Afghanistan rules out the possibility of any integrated Islamic clash with the West. While Afghan warlords affiliated with diverse religious schools fight with each other, they continue to cooperate with the US-led Coalition Force in order to win back American support for retaining control over their respective geographical territories, and for going ahead with their opium cultivation. Thus, the Muslim warlords and the Christian Coalition Force share cooperative relations despite civilizational differences.

Huntington's thesis stands discredited in the light of contradictory historical evidence drawn from 9/11 and its aftermath. Nevertheless, the intellectual explosion caused by his idea continues to capture attention in both the US and Afghanistan. Should Huntington be personally blamed for fuelling the fire of the post-9/11 Afghan war? However, the interpreters can do the damage only when their political interpretations are psychologically received by the masses. How are Huntington's ideas interpreted and received by the Afghans? And how does it affect their collective political lives? These questions can be appropriately responded to by examining the general history of 'political reception' in Afghan politics.

The Afghan History of 'Political Reception': Receiving Huntington

A wide range of opinions cropped up with regard to the popular receptivity of Huntington's thesis. An article published in *The New Criterion* (2009) stated:

> Huntington's thesis is not popular among those who believe that the best way of dealing with a clash of civilizations is to pretend that the clash does not exist. But its pertinence to the West has been glaringly evident since the morning of September 11, 2001.[132]

Acknowledging the significance of Huntington's thesis not only for the West but also for the Muslim world, Said Amir Arjomand observed: 'Huntington's thesis has been quite popular among the Islamic fundamentalists'.[133] K.P. Fabian asked, 'How does one account for the popularity of Huntington's book among the non-specialists and the unprecedented attention it has received from the specialists?'[134] Though the question raised by Fabian has been

---

[132] 'Who are We? On the Passing of Samuel Huntington and The Clash of Civilizations', February 2009, *The New Criterion*, Vol. 27, available at http://www.newcriterion.com/articles.cfm/Who-are-we--4003

[133] Arjomand, Said Amir 'Can Rational Analysis Break a Taboo? A Middle Eastern Perspective' available at http://essays.ssrc.org/sept11/essays/arjomand.htm

[134] Fabian, K. P. 'The Politics of War', *Frontline*, Vol. 19, No. 2, available at http://www.

answered in many ways, Asta Olesen has provided a theoretical and, therefore, generalised understanding of the process of 'political reception'. While discussing the determinants of the reception of a political discourse, Olesen wrote: 'What determines the reception of a political discourse cannot be determined purely based on the content of the discourse in question. Circumstantial factors have a great bearing upon the receptivity and interpretation of the discourse'.[135] Olesen pointed out two determinants - first, the 'content' of the discourse as a product of intellectual 'agency'; second, the 'circumstantial factors' attending the discourse as a factor of intellectual 'structure'. The combination of agency and structure, as stressed by the humanistic-existential model of psychology in the previous chapter, can explain the general history of political reception and the history of Huntington's reception in Afghan politics. But how should the intellectual agency and structure be exercised and evoked by a political discourse to acquire receptivity amongst the Afghans?

Afghan history suggests that any political discourse is psychologically well received by the majority of Afghans if it possesses two features. First, the intellectual agency shapes the content of the discourse in such a way as to make a strong reference to 'Islam'. Second, the intellectual structure, traditionally dominated by the ethnic Pashtuns, finds the discourse politically beneficial for itself. The awakening of Islamic content to derive political benefits for Pashtuns enables any political discourse to capture the 'social imaginary' or what Arkoun calls the 'social imagery' of Afghans. Arkoun opines that any political discourse can reach the majority of the people only if it integrates and articulates the most common and shared ideological elements from the popular traditions or the social imagery, representing a historical continuity outliving any political discourse.[136] Since the prevalence of Islam and the dominance of ethnic Pashtuns mark the historical continuity in Afghan politics, they remain crucial in determining Afghan social imaginary. The historic receptivity or non-receptivity of the political discourses generated by PDPA, Mujahideen and the Taliban/al-Qaida can be explained in terms of their success or failure to capture this Afghan social imaginary.

The content of PDPA discourse was essentially Marxist in character. It placed the 'class struggle' on top of its agenda, thereby initially neglecting any reference to Islam. When the PDPA found it difficult to mobilise the Afghans through an appeal to 'class consciousness', it finally began making appeals to their ethnic, tribal, and regional identities. Olesen interrogated: 'Was the

hindu.com/fline/fl1902/fl190200.htm
[135] Olesen, Asta 1996 *Islam and Politics in Afghanistan*, Curzon Press, p.302.
[136] Arkoun, M. 1988 'The Concept of Authority in Islamic Thought' in Ferdinand K. and Mozaffari, M. (eds.) *Islam, State and Society*, Curzon Press, pp. 53-74.

appeal to Islam and tribal code by the PDPA regime in Afghanistan mere rhetoric and 'window dressing' or did it represent a real attempt at integrating Islamic and tribal elements in the regime's ideological discourse?'[137] Whatever might be the case, Oleson concluded that the PDPA discourse did not manage to command much support on its own because the personal credibility of PDPA leadership, at least as 'good Muslims', was too tainted before they could alter the picture by incorporating the Islamic content in their discourse.[138] The PDPA discourse did not only lack Islamic content, but it also held no promise for political benefit to the structurally dominant group of Pashtuns. The head of the PDPA regime, Babrak Karmal, was a non-Pashtun. Therefore, he was disliked by the Pashtun majority. The Soviets tried to correct this mistake by replacing Karmal with Najibullah, a Pashtun. However, before Najibullah could win widespread support, the PDPA was over-exposed as an organization of infidels. The PDPA regime, which managed to survive for 14 years on the basis of Soviet aid, finally collapsed in 1992 after the withdrawal of Soviet forces from Afghanistan in 1989.

The PDPA regime was followed by Mujahideen rule. In fact, the Mujahideen managed to enter into the political mainstream by exposing the atheism of PDPA and its attachment to the atheistic Soviet Union.[139] In contrast to the attempted imposition of 'Godless' Soviet-style Marxism by the PDPA regime, the Mujahideen claimed to establish an Islamic State of Afghanistan, thereby developing a religiously charged, and therefore, comparatively superior political discourse. The Mujahideen discourse was rich not only in terms of Islamic content but also in terms of its political attractiveness for ethnic Pashtuns. The Mujahideen, whose leaders were highly respected for their religious credentials,[140] were a coalition of seven Sunni groups mostly comprised of Pashtuns, along with some Tajiks, Uzbeks, Hazaras, and Nuristanis. Six of the seven Mujahideen organisations were dominated by Pashtuns.[141]

However, the Mujahideen failed to deliver the promise of clear political benefit to Pashtuns over and above its non-Pashtun members as the latter refused to accept the Pashtun dominance. Moreover, the Mujahideen coalition committed the blunder of excluding a major Pashtun organisation led by Gulbuddin Hikmatyar, thereby further breeding dissatisfaction and division amongst the Pashtun majority. The intra-Pashtun conflict prevented leaders of

[137] Olesen, Asta, op.cit, p.16.
[138] See Sinno, Abdulkader H. 2008 *Organizations at War in Afghanistan and Beyond*, Cornell University Press, p. 166.
[139] Maley, William 'Interpreting the Taliban' in Maley, William (ed.), op.cit, p.8.
[140] Sinno, Abdulkader H., op.cit, p. 126.
[141] Saikal, Amin 2006 *Modern Afghanistan: A History of Struggle and Survival*, I. B. Tauris, p.210.

Pashtun-dominated organisations from taking a united political stand.[142] The moderate Islamism propagated by Mujahideen discourse proved incapable of binding the Pashtuns together, thereby lasting for a brief period of four years and paving the way for the extreme Islamism of the Taliban in 1996.

The Mujahideen's claimed Islamic rule was rapidly upstaged by the Taliban's extremist medievalism in the name of Islam.[143] Highlighting the Islamic appeal of the Taliban/al-Qaida discourse as a major reason behind its immediate popularity, Olivier Roy asserted: 'The rise of the Taliban from 1994 onwards suggests that the appeal of Islam for building a new political order has not faded away.'[144] In line with Roy's assertion, Larry Goodson highlighted the 'religious piety' and 'shared Pashtun ethnicity' of the Taliban as the most telling factors behind its rise.[145] Likewise, Abdulkader H. Sinno opined that any explanation of the rise of the Taliban must explain how they mobilised the Pashtun.[146] The statements of Roy, Goodson and Sinno reveal that the Taliban/al-Qaida discourse not only successfully incorporated a radical Islamic appeal, but also proved politically promising to Pashtuns, thereby satisfying both the criteria for attaining political reception amongst the Afghans. However, what remains unclear in the observations of these scholars is the distinctiveness of the Taliban/al-Qaida discourse that made its Islamic appeal more convincing for the ethnic Pashtuns, than the one presented by its predecessor, the Mujahideen. A comparative study of the 'content/agency' and 'circumstantial factors/structure' of the respective political discourses of the Mujahideen and the Taliban/al-Qaida can contribute some light in this regard.

A comparison of the contents of these discourses discloses the following points of departure. First, the Islamic appeal of the Mujahideen discourse was directed against one country – the Soviet Union, whereas the Islamic appeal of the Taliban/al-Qaida discourse was meant not only to destroy America, but also to attack all Western countries led by the US. Thus, the Taliban/al-Qaida discourse was designed to activate Islam for fighting against a larger and more powerful opposition. Second, the Mujahideen discourse presented the

---

[142] See Shirkogoroff, S. M. 1935 *Psychomental Complex of the Tungus*, Kegan Paul, Trench, Trubner, pp.12-23.
[143] Saikal, Amin, op.cit, p.209.
[144] Olivier Roy in his 1995 work, *The Failure of Political Islam*, Cambridge University Press, argued that Afghan Islamist movements experienced a general decrease of influence. However, in his 1999 work, 'Has Islamism a Future in Afghanistan?', in Maley, William (ed.),op.cit, p. 200, he admits the importance of Islam in shaping Afghan politics.
[145] See Goodson, Larry P. 2001 *Afghanistan's Endless War: State Failure, Regional Politics, and the Rise of the Taliban,* University of Washington Press, pp.109-111.
[146] Sinno, Abdulkader H., op.cit, p. 231.

Soviets as kafirs/infidels/atheists who had little respect for the believers of Islam, whereas the Taliban/al-Qaida discourse projected the Western countries not just as infidels or non-believers, but also as 'Zionist-Crusaders'[147] who were the traditional enemies of the believers of Islam. Therefore, the Taliban/al-Qaida discourse was framed to deal with a more dangerous opposition that was not just disrespectful, but also historically driven by the spirit of animosity against Islam. Third, the Mujahideen discourse sought to mobilise the Afghans bearing diverse ethnic affiliations, whereas the Taliban discourse contained a heavy dose of 'Pashtunwali' and reflected an 'anti-Shiite' orientation, thereby targeting only the Pashtuns, not other ethnic groups, as its potential audience. The Taliban/al-Qaida discourse was more focused and intense in terms of its capacity to attract the structurally dominant group of Pashtuns. Fourth, the Mujahideen discourse tried to direct the Afghans to oust the Soviet-backed regime and establish an Islamic state of Afghanistan, whereas the Taliban/al-Qaida discourse aimed at raising all the believers of Islam, both within and without Afghanistan, to fight for removing Western interference from the internal political affairs of all Muslim states. Unlike the Mujahideen discourse, the Taliban/al-Qaida discourse was more ambitious as it was formulated to conduct a transnational project.

The circumstantial factors attending the two discourses can be compared at two levels – domestic and global. At the domestic level, the situation attending the Mujahideen discourse was marked by the weak political credentials of the Soviet-backed Najibullah regime, whereas the circumstance facing the arrival of the Taliban/al-Qaida discourse was defined by the eroded political legitimacy of mutually warring ethnicities of Mujahideen. In contrast to the Mujahideen discourse, the Taliban/al-Qaida discourse offered greater prospect for political benefit to ethnic Pashtuns as it promised the riddance of, and victory over, not just the foreign Soviet force, but also the domestic non-Pashtun forces comprising the warring factions of Mujahideen. The Taliban/al-Qaida discourse found a ready purchase amongst the Pashtuns, also, because it ignited the hope for resolving their age-old 'Pashtunistan issue', whereby they have been demanding an independent or semi-independent statehood for themselves. In their struggle for Pashtunistan, the Pashtuns have refused to accept the Durand Line laid by the British in 1893 in the middle of the lands of Eastern Pashtuns. They have demanded the return of Pashtuns living in Pakistan to Afghanistan's control, or at least the attainment of autonomy for the claimed region of Pashtunistan. Since the Taliban/al-Qaida discourse was formulated and pursued by the Pashtuns residing on both sides of the Durand Line, it successfully aroused the expectation for transforming the Pashtunistan conflict. The Durand Line has not only affected

---

[147] 'Declaration of War Against the Americans Occupying the Land of the Two Holy Places'; 'Jihad Against Jews and Crusaders', op.cit.

the history of Pashtuns but has also changed their social and economic conditions. So long as the Taliban/al-Qaida discourse manages to maintain the hope for concretising the dream of Pashtunistan, it is likely to retain its appeal amongst Afghans.

At the global level, the Mujahideen discourse emerged when the Soviet Union and its Marxist model of governance was collapsing, whereas the Taliban/al-Qaida discourse originated when the US and its capitalist model of development was being declared as triumphant.[148] While the fragile Soviet opponent of the Mujahideen discourse was already disintegrating, the robust Western enemy of the Taliban/al-Qaida discourse was claiming its everlasting superiority. The comparatively weaker Soviet opponent of the Mujahideen discourse was not stimulating enough to bind the Afghans for long, whereas the hegemonic tendencies of the US has continued to remain sufficiently challenging to provoke an ongoing protest by the Taliban and al-Qaida.

Besides the provocations unleashed from the hegemonic tendencies of the US, the resurgence of Islamic fundamentalism under the leadership of the Taliban and al-Qaida can be attributed to the general decline of secular modernity. Fred Halliday wrote:

> The Islamist movements, although themselves determinedly committed to taking and using state power, are above all revolts against the policies – authoritarian, secular and intrusive – of the modernizing state...The inability of these (secular) states to meet either the economic expectations or the cultural aspirations of their people has provided the context in which Islamist movements have developed.[149]

Against the backdrop of the poor performance of secular states, the alternative model of an 'Islamic state' offered by the Islamist movements easily gained widespread attention. As opposed to secular states, the Islamic states consider the demand for a separation of religion and politics as 'anti-religious'. They seek to express the class war in the name of 'religion', a tendency which the Left has failed to grasp.[150] Until, and unless, the internal problems of these countries are reduced, different variants of Islamism are likely to retain their appeal. It is no wonder that the extreme vision of Islamism propagated by the Taliban/al-Qaida discourse has become immensely popular amongst the Afghans who are disillusioned by the efforts of various Afghan

---

[148] Fukuyama, Francis 1992 *The End of History and the Last Man*, Penguin.

[149] Halliday, Fred p.128.

[150] Khan, Sartaj Summer 2009 'Imperialism, Religion and Class in Swat', *International Socialism*, No. 123, p.26.

modernisers in uplifting their miserable living conditions.

The factors explaining the influential impact of the Taliban/al-Qaida discourse also provide clues for understanding the popularity of Huntington amongst the Afghans. In fact, the discourses generated by the Taliban/al-Qaida and Huntington reflect a striking resemblance. Like the Taliban/al-Qaida discourse, which established the West as the enemy of Islam and was intended to mobilise Muslims around the world to safeguard their pious Islamic lands from Western intervention, the Huntingtonian discourse of civilizational clash inversely matched these propositions by presenting Islam as the most intolerant and aggressive civilization that posed the greatest threat to the West. Huntington advised the West to protect itself from Islamic demons by exploiting the differences between non-Western civilizations and by maintaining the superiority of the West. While the Taliban and al-Qaida appealed for Islamisation, Huntington called for Americanisation.

Both these discourses emerged around the mid-1990s, uttered the language of religious war and fed upon their mutual enmity. The common violent thrusts of both discourses continue to thrive upon their capacity to accept and reinforce each other. Huntington himself admitted this reality in an interview:

> The terrorist actions of Osama bin Laden have reinvigorated civilizational identity. Just as he seeks to rally Muslims by declaring war on the West, he has given back to the West its sense of common identity in defending itself.[151]

However, it cannot and should not be overlooked that the sense of common civilizational identity has better served the interests of the US than that of the Afghans. The civilizational identity emphasised by Huntington has granted the US,

> a profound ideological-political-diplomatic gain by enabling it to subordinate the UN and to create an 'international coalition' of states, many of which are themselves guilty of practicing terrorism. It has also allowed the US to have a military-political entry in Central Asia on a depth and scale that it never before had.[152]

---

[151] Samuel P. Huntington in an interview with Nathan Gardels, op.cit.

[152] Vanaik, Achin 2004 'US Perspectives in a Global and South Asian Context: Before and After 11 September' in Haidar, Salman (ed.) *The Afghan War and its Geopolitical Implications for India*, Manohar, p.119.

By contrast, the activation of civilizational identity by the Taliban and al-Qaida has not been able to deliver anything better than a war-torn inhabitancy for Afghans, where they feel insecure in all possible meanings of the term.

Those Afghans who believe in the Taliban/al-Qaida discourse are bound to succumb to the intellectual insights of Huntington's thesis which endorses the same worldview in a reverse guise. The popularity of al-Zawahiri's text, *Knights Under the Prophet's Banner*[153], that presents a worldview comparable – but in reverse – to Huntington's thesis, supports this argument. The Afghans are trapped in a vicious cycle generated by these two destructive discourses. They have so far been unable to bring an end to their tragic state of affairs and build an alternative theoretical and political discourse for themselves. The lack of an alternative theoretical/political discourse largely accounts for the absence of an alternative and peaceful way of life for Afghans.

---

[153] Kepel, Gilles 2004 The War for Muslim Minds: Islam and the West, Belknap Press, p.99.

4

Critical International Theory: A Comparative Advantage Framework

Huntington's clash of civilizations thesis is marked by obvious limits. However, the task of highlighting flaws in Huntington's thesis is not as significant and desirable as discovering an alternative theoretical framework that is more meritorious in terms of its capability to comprehend social reality. For judging the relative merits of two or more substantive theories making competing claims about social reality, Rosenberg evokes Ian Craib's three criteria.[154] First, the theory must be based on mutually *consistent* propositions. Second, the theory must be measured against *evidence*. Third, the theory must specify in *more detail* the causal processes at work and the situations in which the causal mechanisms come into operation. With respect to Craib's criteria, Critical International Theory (CIT) appears to be promising.

CIT combines two main sets of influences. First, the 'production paradigm' shaped by the work of Antonio Gramsci and introduced into IR by Robert W. Cox. Second, the 'communication paradigm', developed by the Frankfurt School (Habermas, Horkheimer and Adorno) and applied to IR by Andrew Linklater. Though both paradigms share a common ancestry in the Hegelian-Marxist tradition and Kantian tradition of critical philosophy, the Gramscian production paradigm focuses more on economic 'base', whereas the Frankfurtian communication paradigm concentrates more on the ideological 'superstructure'. CIT is often, then, viewed not as an integral whole, but as an amalgam of two distinct paradigms concerning two distinct concepts and processes. The production paradigm tends to focus on the concept of work, and struggles over redistribution. The communication paradigm is concerned with the concept of interaction and identity struggles. Critics argue that neither paradigm is adequate for the task of understanding the problematic of the

---

[154] Rosenberg, Justin 1994 *The Empire of Civil Society*, Verso, p.52.

other.[155] They hold that the *work-interaction divide* is the fundamental problem of CIT.

However, this chapter tries its best to counter this charge. It sets out to forge a strong link between the twin paradigms of CIT. Furthermore, the chapter attempts to find out the points of congruence between CIT and the humanistic-existential model of psychology that constituted the basis of the psychological critique of Huntington's thesis. Ultimately, the chapter aims at establishing CIT as a more commendable theoretical framework than Huntington's clash of civilizations thesis. The chapter is divided into three sections. The first section constructs CIT as a single overarching framework. The second section traces the overlap between the assertions of CIT and the discernments obtained from the humanistic-existential model of psychology. The third section demonstrates the relative strengths of CIT against the weaknesses of the clash of civilizations thesis. The objective of the chapter is to evaluate the conformity of CIT with the two criteria specified by Craib, namely, ensuring internal consistency and providing sufficiently detailed explanation of causal mechanisms. The remaining criterion of measuring the CIT against evidence will be taken up in the next chapter.

The Overarching Framework of CIT: Bridging the Gap

Do we have a singular framework of CIT or are there two distinct paradigms labouring under the label 'critical international theory'? Richard Wyn Jones's probe into this issue led to the conclusion that rather than understanding CIT as a particular approach, it is more appropriate to view it as a constellation of distinctive approaches all seeking to illuminate a central theme – that of *emancipation.*[156] Jones' conclusion presents a fragmented picture of CIT, but assures us that its constitutive paradigms are united, at least in terms of attaining the final objective of emancipation. In fact, the common emancipatory objective emanates from a common broad intellectual project wherein the themes of *hegemony*, *reason* and *transcendence* play a central role.[157] Though the usage of these themes in seemingly distinct paradigms resists reduction to a common denominator, essential core or generative first principle, the themes are, nonetheless, linked in significant ways.[158]

---

[155]   Ibid, p.17.

[156]   Jones, op.cit, p.4.

[157]   Here 'hegemony' implies the Gramscian combination of consent (intellectual and moral leadership) and coercion (sanctions and punishments) whereas 'reason' denotes the Habermasian approximation of mutual understanding (consensus). The term 'transcendence' expresses an urge to surpass the boundaries of the state as the dominant form of political community.

[158]   Jay, Martin 1984 *Adorno,* Fontana Press, p.15.

The hegemonic elements of the production paradigm tend to owe their existence to the virtual speech community of the communication paradigm. Cox explains that *hegemony* derives from the ways of doing and thinking of the dominant strata of the dominant state or states insofar as these ways of doing and thinking have acquired the *acquiescence* of the dominant social strata of other states. The dominant social strata fuse together to compose the hegemonic historic bloc (intellectual and moral bloc). The social practices and the ideologies that *legitimise* the hegemonic historic bloc constitute the formation of a hegemonic order.[159]

The central significance of manufacturing acquiescence and legitimacy in the formation of a hegemonic order makes it difficult to situate its existence entirely within the confines of the production paradigm. The *reason* backing the process of manufacturing acquiescence and legitimacy is largely shaped and contested within the boundaries of the communication paradigm. *The Theory of Communicative Action* (1981/85), in which Habermas engaged with Horkheimer and Adorno's *Dialectic of Enlightenment,* argued that the 'instrumental reason' that necessarily governed the realms of money and power could and should be held in check by a 'communicative reason' welling up from the life-world beyond them, in which action was oriented not to material success but to mutual understanding.[160]

While Cox's understanding of 'production' extends to incorporate ideas, inter-subjective meanings, norms, institutions and social practices within which material goods are produced, Linklater emphasises the extra-material consequences of material dominance by asserting that the material difference in power hinders a genuinely inclusive communication, thereby contributing to the perpetuation of the structures of material dominance. The hegemonic elements of the production paradigm enjoy a greater say in the virtual speech community of the communication paradigm. The exclusion and suppression of the voices of the hegemonised in the communication paradigm are crucial for the survival of the hegemonic elements of the production paradigm. Linklater's realisation that intellectual projects have important moral implications for the national and international distribution of wealth and power, and his call for an inclusive participatory process enabling deliberation about publicly presented arguments and evidence in order to put a curb to the seemingly perpetual structures of material dominance,[161] testify to the *dialectically* inter-woven character of the twin paradigms of CIT. The

[159] Cox, Robert W. 1992 'Towards a Post-hegemonic Conceptualization of World Order' in James N. Rosenau and Ernest Otto-Czempiel (eds.) *Governance Without Government: Order and Change in World Politics,* Cambridge, pp. 132-160.
[160] Anderson, Perry 2005 *Spectrum,* Verso, p.116.
[161] Linklater, Andrew 1998 *The Transformation of Political Community,* Columbia, p.129.

communication paradigm can be simultaneously exploited for pushing, as well as blocking, the ascent of the hegemonic elements of the production paradigm.

The principal battleground over which the struggle for hegemony is now occurring moves beyond the traditional Westphalian states-system.[162] While Linklater draws on Habermasian discourse ethics to *transcend* the logic of the state system, Cox borrows from Gramscian hegemonic and counter-hegemonic discourse to assert that the essential entities of the international system are not just states but also state-society complexes. Acknowledging the role of sub- and trans-state political and economic forces in conditioning the possibilities of international politics,[163] Linklater examines how states can transcend the divisive pursuit of national security by creating an international order, and transform a minimal order between states into a cosmopolitan *community of humankind.*[164] He claims that there have been some conceptions of post-national citizenship that envisage new forms of political community in which state powers are shared with higher and lower authorities and where traditional national loyalties yield to both local and cosmopolitan attachments.[165]

In a similar vein, Cox calls for the need to reconstitute the political authorities at local, national, and global levels and to decipher the 'nebuleuse' of *global economy.*[166] Cox's depiction of global economy as a nebuleuse conjures up an image of a cloud in which there is no centre of power. Multiple state and non-state actors play together to share power in complex ways. Though economic power is becoming more concentrated in the world's major transnational corporations, states remain the cornerstones of global politics. Cox opines that states become more effectively accountable to a nebuleuse personified as global economy and they are constrained to mystify this external accountability in the eyes and ears of their own publics through the new vocabulary of globalisation.[167] Cox visualises the global economy as embedded in global civil society. For him, the global civil society is the emerging international structure of political authority – the 'internationalising of the state', to be the counterpart to the 'internationalising of production' –

---

[162] See Teschke, Benno 2003 *The Myth of 1648*, Verso.

[163] Linklater, Andrew 1990 *Beyond Marxism and Realism: Critical Theory and International Relations*, Macmillan, pp. 1-7.

[164] Linklater, Andrew 1992 'The Question of the Next Stage in International Relations Theory', *Millennium*, Vol.21, No.1, pp. 77-98.

[165] Linklater, Andrew 2008 *Critical Theory and World Politics: Citizenship, Sovereignty and Humanity,* Manohar, p.7.

[166] Cox, Robert W. 2005 'Global Perestroika' in Rorden Wilkinson (ed.), *The Global Governance Reader*, Routledge.

[167] Ibid.

which has at its heart the central governmental agencies of the most important industrialised and industrialising economies, together with key multilateral agencies.

Cox's engagement with global economy and global civil society naturally leads to the operationalisation of Gramscian conceptual categories (historic bloc, hegemony, and the like) at the international level. However, critics hold that the internationalisation of Gramscian conceptual categories by Cox indicates his poor understanding of the historical meaning of Gramsci's work. Randall D. Germain and Michael Kenny stress the paradox that Gramsci, above all a theorist who grappled with the discourses and realities of 'statism' in the early twentieth century, is inappropriately used by Cox to theorise not only the existence of a global civil society *disembedded* from the nation-state, but also a form of hegemony reliant on *transnational* social forces. [168] The problems highlighted by Germain and Kenny are twofold. First, they hold that Gramsci's concepts cannot be meaningfully internationalised because Gramsci was occupied with statism and his idea of civil society was essentially bounded by the parameters of state. Second, they think that Cox's view of global civil society cannot be decoded through Gramsci's method because global civil society is disconnected with the nation-state, whereas Gramsci's method was essentially statist.

An in-depth reading of the writings of CIT suggests that neither Gramsci's idea of civil society strictly coincided with state borders, nor Cox's vision of global civil society, is completely detached from nation-states. Commenting on Gramsci's idea of civil society, Craig Murphy wrote:

> It is the political space and collective institutions in which and through which individuals form political identities…It is the realm of voluntary associations, of the norms and practices which make them possible, and of the collective identities they form, the realm where *I* becomes *we*.[169]

In an increasingly globalised world, the political space and institutions that shape collective political identities, as well as the norms and practices that guide them, are essentially 'global' in character and are no longer determined exclusively by nation-states. Therefore, Gramsci's idea of civil society cannot be meaningfully and wholly conceived in the contemporary world until and

---

[168] Germain, Randall D. and Kenny, Michael 1998 'Engaging Gramsci: International Relations Theory and the New Gramscians' *Review of International Studies*, Vol. 24, pp. 3-21.
[169] Murphy, Craig 1994 *International Organization and Industrial Change*, Cambridge, pp.31.

unless it is dragged beyond the traditional limits of 'statism'. In other words, one has to situate the Gramscian notion of civil society in the arena that transcends state borders in order to make sense of it in the contemporary context. However, crossing the traditional limits of statism does not imply abandoning nation-states. While Cox goes beyond statism in conceptualising a global civil society or an 'internationalised state', he does not lose touch with the nation-state altogether. The global civil society, according to him, is inclusive of nation-states, along with other actors like transnational corporations and multilateral agencies. Though Cox admits that global civil society or the internationalised state lacks an explicit political or authority structure, he asserts that it has a specific *modus operandi* that must be the target for continuing analysis.[170] Cox's global civil society has a striking resemblance with Linklater's community of mankind, as both reflect a cosmopolitan outlook.

Like Cox and Linklater, the 'globality' of human social relations as the largest constitutive framework of all contemporary relations has been highlighted by Martin Shaw and William I. Robinson. According to Shaw, in the 'global' epoch, state relations have ceased to be 'national' and 'international' in the historical sense. They have begun to coalesce around a core of *world state institutions,* a progression towards a global state which represents the institutional expressions of state relations along global lines.[171] Similarly, Robinson visualises the emergence of a multi-layered and multi-centred *transnational state apparatus* that functionally interconnects an array of supranational, regional, and national organisations. He believes that the nation-state as a functional component of the transnational state apparatus is not withering away, but is an active agent of global capital.[172] However, Alexander Anievas points out the theoretical vulnerability of Shaw and Robinson.[173] Anievas argues that Shaw's 'globality' fails to demonstrate the effect of global economic processes on the nation-state and on the relations between state managers and capitalists, whereas Robinson's 'transnational state apparatus' entertains a flawed presumption that there is no non-identity of interests between capitalists and state managers. Contrary to the assertions of Robinson, Anievas suggests that global capital is not a homogeneous, but a heterogeneous, category. The problems pointed out by Anievas in the works of Shaw and Robinson are absent in the theoretical

---

[170] See Robert W. Cox and Michael G. Schechter 2002 *The Political Economy of a Plural World: Critical Reflections on Power, Morals and Civilization,* Routledge, p.83.

[171] Shaw, Martin 2000 *Theory of the Global State: Globality as an Unfinished Revolution,* Cambridge University Press, p.17.

[172] Robinson, William I. 2004 *A Theory of Global Capitalism: Production Class and the State in a Transnational World,* John Hopkins university Press, p. 102-110.

[173] Anievas, Alexander 2008 Review Articles, *Historical Materialism,* Vol. 16, pp. 167-236.

framework offered by Cox.

Acknowledging the interdependence of state activities and economic processes, Cox wrote:

> The ideas and material conditions are always bound together, mutually influencing one another, and not reducible one to the other...the juxtaposition and reciprocal relationships of the political, ethical and ideological spheres of activity avoid reductionism.[174]

He further asserted:

> Three categories of forces interact in a structure: material capabilities, ideas and institutions. No one way determinism need be assumed among the three; the relationship can be assumed to be reciprocal.[175]

The enmeshing of the political and economic processes in Cox's theoretical framework provides ample scope for understanding the mutually conflictive and cooperative relationship between capitalists and state managers. While admitting the clash within global capital, Cox stated:

> I don't think of transnational capitalist class as a kind of conspiratorial, unified group, and nor do they, because their whole thesis is that the initiative of the individual organisations and groups is what drives globalization, not some overall strategy... In other words, they want to organise the world in such a way that the conditions for globalization will go on, but the process itself is not something that is masterminded from the top.[176]

As opposed to Alex Callinicos, who borrows Vivek Chibber's term 'soft-functionalism' to explain the existence of the state-system in terms of the

---

[174] Cox, Robert W. 1996 *Approaches to World Order*, Cambridge university Press, p.131.

[175] Cox, Robert. W. 1986 'Social forces, States and World Orders: Beyond International Relations Theory' in Keohane, Robert O. (ed.) *Neo-realism and its Critics,* Columbia University Press, p. 218.

[176] Dale, Roger and Robertson, Susan 2003 'Interview with Robert W. Cox', *Globalisation, Societies and Education* available at http://seriesofhopes.files.wordpress. com/2008/05/interview-cox.pdf

needs of capital,[177] Cox demonstrates a flexible attitude by giving importance to both geopolitics and global economics, without assigning greater weight to either. The flexibility of Cox has been labelled by John M. Hobson as 'collapsed base-structuralism', wherein no causal hierarchy is specified while determining the contribution of economic base and ideological superstructure in shaping the world order. Hobson criticises Cox for being inconsistent in his attempt to mix and match his commitment to 'collapsed base structuralism' with his adherence to the 'relative autonomy approach'.

While the idea of 'collapsed base structuralism' refuses to grant primary importance either to state or to economy, the 'relative autonomy' approach grants more autonomy to the state in shaping economic affairs. Cox's simultaneous commitment to both is ontologically problematic for Hobson.[178] However, Hobson's problem derives from his failure to grasp the nuances of Cox's theoretical strategy, wherein 'synchronic' moments of analysis are combined with the 'diachronic' moments. While the synchronic moments create room for a greater role of the state in regulating economic affairs in the short run, the diachronic moment refuses to assign more importance either to state or to economy while acknowledging the contribution of both. Thus, Hobson's criticism is addressed when one views the possible emergence of the relative autonomy of the state as a short-lived moment in the overall approach of collapsed base-structuralism.

The constructivist vision of hegemony, reason, and transcendence, nurtured by both paradigms of CIT, reveals their common methodological base. The base is firmly rooted in post-positivism as it undertakes a dynamic view of ontology, unlike the hypostatised picture offered by positivism. Cox's understanding of ideas as an inherent part of reality enables him to declare that theory is always for someone and some purpose.[179] Cox's declaration finds echo in Linklater's rejection of the notion that there can be such a thing as a politically neutral analysis of political reality.[180] Their shared scepticism towards deterministic and ahistorical theories allows them to critically analyse the process of theorising itself and to entail a more empowering self-understanding in which humans are actively self-constitutive in the process of

---

[177] For details see Callinicos, Alex 2007 'Does Capitalism Need the State System?', *Cambridge Review of International Affairs,* Vol. 20, No. 4, pp. 533-549.

[178] Hobson, John M. 2010 'To Be or Not to Be a Non-reductionist Marxist: Is that the Question?' in Anievas, Alexander (ed.) *Marxism and World Politics,* Routledge, p. 122.

[179] Cox, Robert W. 1981 'Social Forces, States and World Order: Beyond International Relations Theory', *Millennium,* Vol.10, No.2, pp. 126-155.

[180] Linklater, Andrew 1996 'The Achievements of Critical Theory', in S. Smith, K. Booth and M. Zalewski (eds.) *International Theory: Positivism and Beyond,* Cambridge, pp. 279-298.

consciously reconstructing their internal relations with society and nature.[181] Their profound trust in the potentialities of human agency and their sensitivity towards the vulnerabilities of the structural impediments blend well with the insights of the humanistic-existential model of psychology.

CIT and the Humanistic-Existential Model: Mapping the Overlap

The ontology, or the set of shared meanings, that come to define reality is perceived by the humanistic-existential model of psychology as a mental construct shaped by two mutually contradictory forces. The first is the free *agency* of humans that assigns meaning to a seemingly meaningless world. The second is the *structure* of existence that conditions the free agency and influences the process of meaning-making. The interplay of agency and structure characterises the collective understanding of ontology at different historical junctures. Such an approach to ontology finds resonance in CIT. Cox writes that ontologies are the parameters of our existence.[182] Endorsing Vico's view, he argues that reality is constructed by human minds which in turn are shaped by the complex of social relations. Linklater admits that the capacities of human minds are linked inextricably with the forms of life in which they are involved.[183] The modifications of human minds are identical with human history and therefore ontologies are not arbitrary constructions, but the specifications of the common sense of an epoch.[184]

Four lessons can be drawn from this common line of thinking that underpins CIT and the humanistic-existential model of psychology. First, the ontology is constructed *collectively*, not individually. Second, the ontology exists in *plurality*, not singularity. Third, the process of establishing a dominant ontology[185] is marked by *contestation*, not unanimity. Fourth, the dominant ontology is *dynamic*, not static.

Sterling-Folker holds that meaning making is not an individual or random

---

[181] Gill, Stephen 1993 'Epistemology, Ontology and the Italian School' in Stephen Gill (ed.) *Gramsci, Historical Materialism and International Relations*, Cambridge, p.24.

[182] Cox, Robert W. and Sinclair, Timothy (eds.) 1996 *Approaches to World Order,* Cambridge, p.92.

[183] Linklater, Andrew 2000 'Men and Citizens in International Relations' in Andrew Linklater (ed.) *International Relations: Critical Concepts in Political Science,* Vol. 5, Routledge, p.1842.

[184] Cox, Robert W. *'Critical Political Economy'*, lecture given to the United Nations University conference on Emerging Trends in Political Economy and International Relations Theory, Oslo, Norway, August 1993, p.5.

[185] The term 'dominant ontology' implies a set of shared meanings which is forged by the hegemonic elements of a particular historical structure.

activity.[186] The inter-subjective or collective level of ontological selection transcends individual choice. The collective human responses to material conditions of existence constitute ontology. Once the ontology is constituted, it is reproduced even if we do not approve of it. Cox writes, 'Knowing them (ontologies) to be there means knowing that other people will act as though they are there.'[187]

However, there are variations in the conditions of existence and in the collective human responses to them. Consequently, what emerges is not a single ontology but plural ontologies. Linklater writes,

> Humanity is revealed in the various, if not infinite, human expressions which could be discerned only through observation of what men have unfolded in their diverse cultural contexts. No single culture could manifest the totality of human possibilities.[188]

The 'limited totalities', as Cox calls them, do not incorporate everything, but rather represent a particular sphere of human activity in its historically located totality.

The constitutive factors of the limited totalities or ontologies originate from diverse conditions of existence and compete with each other to acquire the status of the dominant ontology at a particular historical conjuncture. The ontology that succeeds in effectively manipulating the *contradictory consciousness* to win acquiescence and legitimacy becomes the dominant ontology. The dominant ontology may acquire a degree of autonomy, take on its own life, and serve as an agent of change. As Cox puts it, to qualify as ontology, it has to show the interactive properties of a system – albeit an open system in which the homeostatic mechanisms that maintain closure can be disrupted by forces that open the way for change.[189]

Thus, no dominant ontology lasts forever. The dominant ontology and its corresponding historical structure present a simplified representation of a complex reality and an expression of tendencies, limited in their applicability

---

[186] Sterling-Folker, Jennifer 2008 'Postmodern and Critical Theory Approaches' in Jennifer Sterling-Folker (ed.) *Making Sense of International Relations Theory,* Lynne Reinner Publishers, p.159.

[187] Cox, *'Critical Political Economy'*, p.4.

[188] Linklater, '*Men and Citizens in International Relations*', p.1843.

[189] Cox, Robert W. 'The Way Ahead: Toward a New Ontology of World Order' in Jones, p.46.

in time and space, rather than fully realised developments.[190] The clash of rival collective images provides evidence of the potential for alternative paths of development and raises questions as to the possible material and institutional basis for the emergence of an alternative structure.[191] The *diachronic* nature of ontology which is essentially characterised by a tussle between structure (understood as ways of understanding the world as it is) and agency (conceived as the forces that change structures), means there is a propelling force that grants ontology a dynamic status.

This understanding of ontology as a collective, pluralised, contested, and dynamic enterprise enables CIT to enjoy a comparative advantage over Huntington's clash of civilizations thesis. It allows CIT not only to expose the inadequacies, deceits and hypocrisies of Huntington's thesis, but also emerges as a more consistent and comprehensive alternative theoretical framework.

CIT and the Clash of Civilizations Thesis: Tracing the Comparative Edge

The comparative edge of CIT against the clash of civilizations thesis can be traced to its superior methodological base. In contrast to the post-positivist tilt of CIT, the positivist methodology of Huntington mistakenly treats ontology not as a dynamic construct but as a static entity which is essentially deterministic, ahistorical and immobile. Therefore, for Huntington, the dominant ontology that supports the notion of a prospective clash of civilizations is not an outcome of the *time and space sensitive* contestation between diverse collective human responses to varied conditions of existence but a temporally and spatially neutral observation that must be passively accepted. The recognition that temporality and spatiality have varied across periods and cultures, the realisation that they have been socially constructed and mentally experienced in different ways, and those different ways have been highly consequential for the constitution of social orders (social realities) – all of this has been well and long established.[192] Yet, Huntington turns a blind eye to the temporal and spatial dimensions while commenting on the social reality. In other words, the historically and geographically determined causal mechanisms underlying the dominant ontology of civilizational clash remain undiagnosed by Huntington.

This technical mistake accounts for a serious ethical failure. In the process of taking the dominant ontology of civilizational clash as granted, Huntington ends up *reinforcing* a conflictive world order rather than explaining it. What

---

[190] Cox, '*Social Forces, States and World Order*', p.137.
[191] Ibid, pp. 126-155.
[192] Rosenberg, Justin, 2000, *The Follies of Globalization Theory*, Verso, p.4.

presents itself initially as the *explanandum* – the world order fraught with a civilizational clash as the developing outcome of some historical process (i.e. the end of the ideological clash associated with the Cold War) – is progressively transformed into the *explanan* as it is the civilizational clash which now explains the changing character of the world order and informs the foreign policy orientation of the states that wish to survive within it. The chances of surpassing this hellish state of affairs are totally circumscribed by Huntington.

Was the mistaken treatment of ontology by Huntington accidental or intentional? While responding to this pertinent question, CIT would certainly argue that Huntington's mistake was intentional as theories were always meant for serving particular purposes. Critics who do not subscribe to CIT consider Huntington's mistake as accidental and therefore begin with finding fault in the epistemology (realist, orientalist and elitist) and/or methodology (monolithic, inconsistent and reductionist/essentialist) of the clash of civilizations thesis, rather than attacking its unethical premise (purposeful and self-fulfilling orientation). CIT would uncover the hidden purposeful designs of Huntington and his supporters and argue that the acceptance of his thesis is at least partly an outcome of personal motivations. However, the achievements of CIT would not be restricted to pinpointing the technical and ethical deficits of Huntington's thesis. CIT would bank upon its post-positivist orientation to overcome the methodological deficiencies of Huntington's thesis and carve out an alternative that is technically efficient and ethically sound.

The technical efficiency and ethical soundness of CIT germinate from its flexible theoretical tool that ensures two facilities. First, it combines the moments of 'synchronic' and 'diachronic' analysis to provide a time and space sensitive explanation of the social reality. The moment of synchronic analysis critically evaluates the coherence of a social order within its own terms, thereby engaging with the temporally and spatially abstracted aspects of the social reality. The moment of diachronic analysis identifies the contradictions and conflicts in a social order and speculates on the nature and extent of structural change that is feasible, thereby placing the variables of time and space at the centre of the social reality.

The unique combination of the synchronic and diachronic moments of analysis has ethical implications. While the synchronic analysis has status-quo tendencies as it intends to correct the problems of the existing social order while retaining its base, the addition of the diachronic analysis to it allows for a normative choice in favour of a social and political order different from the prevailing order.[193] The synchronic analysis can be utilised for

---

[193] Cox, Robert W. 'Social Forces, States and World Order', pp.129-130.

searching the scope of improving the existing social order in the short run whereas the diachronic analysis can pave the way for a gradual movement towards an alternative social order in the long run. As such, CIT proves useful not only in grasping the evolution of an ever-changing social order but also in *influencing* and *channelling* the process of social change.[194]

Moreover, CIT's move towards a new social order is not motivated by the idea of serving narrow self-interests but a broad humane interest in enlightenment and emancipation.[195] Contrary to the immutability associated with Huntington's thesis, CIT puts forward an emancipatory claim that affirms the human capacity to learn from harmful experiences.[196] The emancipatory claim of CIT is both constitutive and prescriptive. Linklater writes,

> This is partly a constitutive claim; to follow such a path is to become civil. But as with any constitutive claims, it is also a prescriptive one; it suggests a path that the agents [of change] need to follow to form a more civil social environment.[197]

CIT intends to move on to a new social order wherein it is possible to free ourselves from the problematic social structures that cause war, human rights violations, racism, poverty, and so on.[198] By relentlessly focusing on the question of emancipation and by questioning what this might mean in terms of the theory and practice of world politics, CIT successfully crosses the Huntingtonian limits to a desirable social transformation that may be instrumental in building a peaceful world order.

Second, unlike Huntington's thesis, CIT does not convert the explanan into explanandum and therefore is free from the guilt of what Rosenberg calls 'empty circularity'[199]. For Huntington, the post-Cold War world is the explanandum (i.e. the phenomena that needs to be explained in terms of an outcome of some reason) and the notion of civilizational clash is the explanan

---

[194] Cox, Robert W. *'Globalization, Multilateralism and Democracy'*, the John Holmes Memorial Lecture delivered to the conference of the Academic Council of the United States System, Washington D.C., June, 1992.

[195] Bernstein, R. 1976, *The Restructuring of Social and Political Theory*, Oxford and McCarthy, T., 1978, *The Critical Theory of Jürgen Habermas*, Cambridge.

[196] See Linklater, Andrew 2006 'The Harm Principle and Global Ethics', *Global Society*, Vol. 20, No. 3, pp.329-343.

[197] Linklater, Andrew and Suganami, Hidemi 2006 *The English School of International Relations: A Contemporary Reassessment*, Cambridge, p.266.

[198] Wendt, Alexander 'What is International Relations For? Notes Toward a Postcritical View' in Jones, op.cit, p.212.

[199] Rosenberg, Justin *The Follies of Globalization Theory,* p.2.

(i.e. the reason that is used for explaining the phenomena). Since Huntington does not delve deeper into the causal mechanisms that activate the notion of civilizational clash (explanan), it becomes a baseless assertion. Huntington uses this baseless assertion to explain the conflictive character of the post-Cold War world (explanandum). Since the reason of civilizational clash also becomes its outcome, that is the post-Cold War world fraught with civilizational tensions, Huntington's thesis falls into the trap of empty circularity. In order to avoid the empty circularity, Rosenberg recommends that the explanation must fall back on some more basic social theory which could clarify as to why the phenomenon which is being explained became such a distinctive and salient feature of the contemporary world. In the context of Huntington's thesis, CIT can serve as the more basic social theory which can explain why the phenomenon of 'civilizational clash' gained momentum in the present era. The production paradigm can throw light on the disguised political and economic factors working behind what appears as the 'civilizational conflict', while the communication paradigm can reveal the concealed impact of the distortions in the civilizational dialogue on the aggravation of the so-called 'civilizational tensions'.

On the basis of the insights drawn from this theoretical tool, CIT can take a step further in the direction of formulating a *practical agenda* for socio-political transformation and emancipation. Richard Wyn Jones stresses the practical intent of CIT by stating that its willingness to face up to reality simultaneously includes a commitment to its transformation and a belief that such a transformation is feasible. Following Marx, critical theorists seek to understand the world in order to change it.[200] They use different metaphors to express their thrust for practical change. Goodin calls it 'constitutional design' while Turner calls it 'social engineering'.[201] It is 'evolutionary guidance' for Banathy, 'system steering' for Luhmann and 'collective character planning' for Elster.[202] All the critical theorists attempt to identify the sources of potentially far-reaching change so that human subjects can grasp the possibility of alternative paths of historical development which can be explored through collective political action.[203]

---

[200] Jones, Richard Wyn 1999 *Security, Strategy and Critical Theory,* Lynne Reinner Publishers, p.22.

[201] See Robert Goodin (ed.) 1996 *The Theory of Institutional Design,* Cambridge and Jonathan Turner 1998 'Must Sociological Theory and Sociological Practice Be So Far Apart?: A Polemical Answer', *Sociological Perspectives,* Vol. 41, pp.243-258.

[202] See Bela Banathy 1998 'Evolution Guided by Design: A Systems Perspective', *Sysytems Research and Behavioral Science,* Vol.15, pp.161-172; Niklas Luhmann 1997 'Limits of Steering', *Theory, Culture and Society* , Vol.14, No.1, pp.41-57 and Jon Elster 1983 *Sour Grapes,* Cambridge.

[203] Linklater, Andrew and Burchill, Scott (eds.) 1996 *Theories of International Relations,* Macmillan, pp.283-284.

In seeking to identify and promote the potential sites for change, the production paradigm encourages counter-hegemonic political and social movements while the communication paradigm focuses on unrestrained and undistorted discourse. The production paradigm raises a voice against the adverse effects of the globalisation of relations of production on the distribution of the world's wealth. Cox argues that the *Global Perestroika* (i.e. globalisation) that penetrates the totality of structures constituting the present world order can be effectively countered by a challenge at several levels, by a Gramscian 'war of position' of probably a long duration.[204] While drawing a rough sketch of the principles required for initiating such a war of position, he writes:

> The movement presupposes the rediscovery of social solidarity and of confidence in a potential for sustained collective creativity, inspired by a commitment to social equity, to reciprocal recognition of cultural and civilizational differences, to biospheric survival, and to non-violent methods of dealing with conflict. The supreme challenge is to build a counter-hegemonic formation that would embody these principles; and this task implies as a first step the working out of an ontology that focuses attention on the key elements in this struggle.[205]

The task of framing an ontology that is conducive to Cox's principles of counter-hegemonic movement can be concretised by approximating, if not establishing, Linklater's 'ideal speech community' which ensures the inclusive participation of all the hitherto suppressed voices in the collective process of ontology framing. The inputs from the counter-hegemonic forces in the collective process of ontology framing would involve the unpacking or pulling apart of meanings embedded or implicitly assumed in the dominant texts, whether these texts are public statements by policymakers or the writings of other IR scholars.[206] By pulling apart meaning-making it is possible not only to reveal the knowledge-producing power structures underneath,[207] but to produce alternative knowledge-producing structures backed by the counter-hegemonic consensus. The alternative knowledge-producing structures can

---

[204] For Gramsci, the war of position was analogous to 'trench warfare', whereas the 'war of movement' meant 'frontal attack'. For a nuanced analysis of these concepts see Anderson, Perry 1976 'The Antinomies of Antonio Gramsci', *New Left Review,* Vol.1, No. 100.

[205] Cox, 'The Way Ahead: Toward a New Ontology of World Order' in Jones, op.cit, p.59.

[206] See Selby, Jan 2007 'Engaging Foucault: Discourse, Liberal Governance, and the Limits of Foucauldian IR', *International Relations,* Vol. 21, No. 3, pp. 324-345.

[207] Sterling-Folker, op.cit, p.160.

provide a sustained boost to the counter-hegemonic movement in the long run.

Though Marc Lynch believes that a focus on communication can act as a possible site for foundational knowledge-claims and the practical achievement of emancipation,[208] Stephen Leonard has rightly observed that forging a link between social theory and political practice is no mean task.[209] The task becomes all the more complicated because it involves uniquely difficult and essentially epistemological issues of 'rationality'. Though the 'ideal speech condition' emits a hope that the collective outcomes would be determined not by the considerations of power, social identities, or cultural distortions but by the supreme force of rationality, the notion of rationality remains both theoretically and practically problematic. Alexander Wendt writes, 'If the present is complex and the future radically uncertain, then it is not clear what rationality even means, let alone what rational choices should be'.[210] However, Wendt's statement is indicative of the fact that our choices are *rationally* determined and our rationality is *temporally* contingent. As such, the theoretical issue of conceptualising rationality and the related practical challenge of making rational choices become open to contestation by the collectivities that are the peculiar 'products' as well as 'producers' of their own time. It is CIT that sets the stage for such a contestation, not the clash of civilizations thesis which, in its quest for maintaining the status-quo, deliberately refuses to speak to this problem.

The outcome of the contestation of rationality facilitated by CIT might seem inconclusive in the short run, but its pursuance as an ongoing project in the long run guarantees a safeguard against the silent acceptance of an 'uncontested irrationality' masquerading as what appears as rationality. After all, the idea of contesting (ir)rationality is rational for all as it promises to unleash an emancipatory effect. The American poet, A. R. Ammons, endorses a similar view when he quotes: 'Definition, rationality, and structure are ways of seeing, but they become prisons when they blank out other ways of seeing'.[211] The basic attraction of CIT over and above the clash of civilizations thesis lies in its propensity to break free from those prisons.

It is true that the theoretical superiority of CIT cannot be established merely at the methodological level. Craib is right in his opinion that the testing of theory

---

[208] Lynch, Marc 2006 *Voices of the New Arab Public: Iraq, Al-Jazeera and Middle East Politics Today*, Columbia.
[209] Leonard, Stephen T. 1990 *Critical Theory in Political Practice,* Princeton, p.3.
[210] Wendt, 'What is International Relations For? Notes Toward a Postcritical View' in Jones, op.cit, p.207.
[211] Hall, Donald (ed.) 1982 *Claims for Poetry,* University of Michigan Press, p. 4.

against evidence is crucial. The lack of evidence in support of a theory renders its methodological edge inconsequential. Moreover, the potential of a methodologically superior theory can be fully tapped only when it helps to see what is glaringly evident but deliberately overlooked. The meeting of theoretical methodology with practical evidence is immensely decisive for the agenda of emancipation. The next chapter is in sync with this idea as it centres its scope on the meeting of CIT with the evidence drawn from post-9/11 Afghanistan.

5

An Alternative Understanding of Post-9/11 Afghanistan: The Critical-Theoretical Perspective

The theoretical superiority of Critical International Theory (CIT) over the clash of civilizations thesis can be confirmed by employing CIT to provide an alternative and comparatively more accurate portrayal of post-9/11 Afghanistan. The insights offered by the dual paradigms of CIT – namely, 'production' and 'communication' as developed by Robert W. Cox and Andrew Linklater respectively - can be utilised for capturing the complex dynamics of post-9/11 Afghan politics. Cox's production paradigm can throw light on the historical process of the hegemonisation of Afghan society. Linklater's communication paradigm can identify the historical moments of rupture or distortion in dialogue between 'the Islamists' and 'the West' on the one hand and between different ethnic groups of Afghanistan on the other. The combined application of both the paradigms constituting the overarching framework of CIT can reveal the linkage between hegemonic shifts and dialogic tensions in Afghan politics. By testing the assertions of CIT against the practical evidence drawn from post-9/11 Afghanistan, this chapter aims at unfolding the genealogy of the current Afghan crisis, thereby providing an alternative understanding that takes into account the temporal and spatial dimensions of social reality. The alternative understanding constructs the post-9/11 Afghan scenario not as an instance of clash of civilizations, but as a clash of hegemonic aspirations.

The objective of the chapter is not exhausted by offering an alternative understanding. On the basis of the alternative understanding gained from the application of CIT, the chapter goes further to design a preliminary agenda for transforming the post-9/11 Afghan crisis. In this endeavour, the production paradigm facilitates an assessment of the actual and potential role of contemporary counter-hegemonic forces active in Afghanistan. The communication paradigm shows some directions to approximate, if not establish, the 'ideal speech community' which in turn might prove helpful in strengthening the counter-hegemonic forces. The chapter concludes that the shifting of perspective from 'civilizational' to 'critical' not only presents a finer vision of the post-9/11 Afghan crisis but also suggests a way out of it. The chapter is divided into three sections. The first section activates Cox's production paradigm to demonstrate the hegemonic shifts in Afghan politics. The second section operationalises Linklater's communication paradigm to trace the linkage of these hegemonic shifts with the dialogic tensions in Afghan society. Finally, the third section sets out to recommend critical solutions to so-called 'civilizational' problems in post-9/11 Afghanistan.

Marking the Hegemonic Shifts

Robert W. Cox firmly rejects the label 'Marxist' and claims to merely apply to the study of international relations ideas derived from a selective reading of Gramsci's *Prison Notebooks* – of which the most important is the concept of 'hegemony'.[212] Hegemony implies the art of providing 'intellectual and moral leadership'[213] through a peculiar combination of 'coercion' and 'consent'. The exceeding coercive force and shrinking consensual basis are viewed as symptoms of decline in hegemony. Cox writes: 'The more the military force has to be increased and the more it is actually employed, the less the world order rests on consent and the less it is hegemonic'.[214] For analysing the coercive and consensual mechanisms of hegemony, Cox enumerates three spheres of activities: social relations of production, forms of state and world orders.

The *social relations of production* cover the production and reproduction of knowledge and of the social relations, morals, and institutions that are prerequisites to the production of physical goods.[215] This broader understanding of production ensures that social forces are not reduced to the economic substratum. The 'non-class' dimensions of peace and ecology are to be given a crucial space in social realities shaped through the production process. The *forms of state* rest on underlying configurations of forces rooted in civil society.[216] Different forms of state are expressions of particular

---

[212] Budd, Adrian 2007 'Gramsci's Marxism and International Relations', *International Socialism*, Issue 114, available at http://www.isj.org.uk/index.php4?id=309&issue=114
[213] Gramsci, 1971 *Selections from Prison Notebooks*, translated & edited by Quintin Hoare and Geoffrey Nowell Smith, International Publishers, p.182.
[214] Cox, Robert W. 1987 *Production, Power and World Order: Social Forces in the Making of History*, p.289.
[215] Ibid, p. 1-9.
[216] See Gramsci, op.cit, p.261.

'historical blocs' that emerge from the way in which leading social forces within a specific national context establish dominance[217] over contending social forces, thereby establishing an organic link between political and civil society.[218] The integration of diverse social forces constituting the historical bloc brings about not only a unison of economic and political aims, but also of intellectual and moral dispositions. The *world orders* originate from the historical blocs that initially consolidate themselves at the national level but later spread outward on a world scale through the international expansion of a particular mode of social relations of production. Within each sphere of activity, the three elements reciprocally combine to constitute a hegemonic order: ideas (inter-subjective meanings as well as collective images of world order), material capabilities, and institutions claiming universality. A hegemonic world order therefore is the product of a universal society and civilisation[219] that successfully forms an international historical bloc of social forces that in turn is premised upon the global 'reception' of a dominant form of knowledge.

Since the 'social forces'[220] are the most elementary and influential factors in shaping hegemony, the rise of contending social forces aiming at replacing the dominant form of knowledge and the related social relations of production, may generate mutually reinforcing transformations in the forms of state and world order, thereby heralding a counter-hegemonic order. The idea of a counter-hegemonic struggle – advancing alternatives to the dominant form of knowledge – has contributed to the belief that knowledge is a social construct that serves to legitimise (or delegitimise) hegemonic social structures. Cox writes:

> Hegemony consists in the formation of a coalition of top-down forces activated by a common consciousness in which those at the bottom are able to participate. Counter-hegemony arises when bottom-up forces achieve a common consciousness that is clearly distinct from that of hegemonic power. So, a strategy

---

[217] See Cox, Robert W. 1981 'Social Forces, States and World Orders', *Millennium,* Vol.10, No.2, p. 139.
[218] Cox, Robert W. and Sinclair, Timothy J. 1996 *Approaches to World Order,* Cambridge University Press, p. 141.
[219] Cox, Robert W. 1992 'Towards a Post-hegemonic Conceptualization of World Order: Reflections on the Relevance of Ibn Khaldun' in Rosenau, James N. and Czempiel, Ernest-Otto (eds.) *Governance without Government: Order and Change in World Politics,* Cambridge University Press, p. 141.
[220] Cox divides social forces into two categories. The social forces that operate from the top-down are those that try to maintain the trajectory of existing power relations, whereas the social forces that operate from bottom-up are those that tend to challenge the existing power relations.

of structural transformation may be seen as a project for the formation of counter-hegemony.[221]

The 'war of attack' can only succeed with a prior 'war of position' in the form of struggle over ideas and beliefs. Thus, the production of an alternative knowledge-base is essential for forming counter-hegemony.

However, the task of forming counter-hegemony becomes particularly challenging due to complex mediations in the regular consensual and coercive mechanisms of hegemony. Gramsci warns:

> Between consent and force stands corruption/fraud (which is characteristic of certain situations when it is hard to exercise the hegemonic function, and when the use of force is too risky). This consists in procuring the demoralisation and paralysis of the antagonist (or antagonists) by buying its leaders – either covertly, or, in case of imminent danger, openly – in order to sow disarray and confusion in its ranks.[222]

Cox puts these clandestine and corrupt political practices under the label 'the covert world', which includes intelligence agencies, organised crime and the drug trade, money-laundering banks, the arms trade, and terrorist organisations.[223] Cox includes terrorist organisations committed to destroying the existing order amongst the set of forces that have the consequence of maintaining the status quo because at times the terrorist organisations act in cooperation, as well as in conflict, with them.

Though the confusion created by these secret and fraudulent activities weakens the counter-hegemonic drive, it is the '*contradictory consciousness*' that compels the bottom-up forces to demonstrate their autonomous opposition to hegemony, regardless of the barriers created by their own conformist attitude that stems from their urge to fulfil immediate necessities.[224]

---

[221] Cox, Robert W. 2001 'The Way Ahead: Toward a New Ontology of World Order' in Jones, Richard Wyn *Critical Theory and World Politics*, Lynne Reinner, p.56.

[222] Gramsci, op.cit, p.80.

[223] Cox, 2001, op.cit, p.56.

[224] Cox claims that the globalisation of production is producing a three-part social hierarchy. The first level includes those people who are integrated into the global economy in a privileged manner. The second level is composed of those people who serve the global economy in a subordinate way. The third level comprises those people who are excluded from the global economy and are either permanently unemployed or underemployed. While the first level is doing quite well and the second level is expanding most rapidly, it is the third level that poses a potential threat to the

The contradictory consciousness motivates bottom-up forces to work to bring an end to the temporary coalition of diverse hegemonic social forces. However, the bottom-up forces operate within the boundaries of 'historical necessity' or the limits set by the dialectics of a given social structure. As Marx pointed in *The Eighteenth Brumaire* – 'Men make their own history but not in the circumstances of their own choosing'[225] – the social structure both constrains and constitutes social action. Nevertheless, social action can have a transformative impact upon its constraining structure. The exercise of counter-hegemonic agency by bottom-up forces can ultimately lead to the transformation of the hegemonic structure.[226] The domain of politics is all about forming and countering hegemony.

The Coxian vision of politics as a (counter) hegemonic struggle can serve as a meaningful tool to decode the political developments in post-9/11 Afghanistan. For activating the Coxian theoretical scheme in order to mark the hegemonic shifts in post-9/11 Afghan politics, one needs to raise two questions: First, how did specific historical moments in national and global politics (structure) and collective human responses to them (agency) encourage temporary coalitions of diverse hegemonic social forces in Afghanistan? Second, how did the inherent contradictions in these hegemonic coalitions emerge, thereby historically transforming Afghan politics from one hegemonic phase to another? Since the post-9/11 Afghan scenario is largely a culmination of political events that began with the Soviet occupation of Afghanistan in the late 1970s, it is essential to situate the above-mentioned questions against that historical backdrop.

The Soviet intervention in Afghanistan had a destabilising impact on both national (Afghan) politics and global politics. Its atheistic orientation threatened the hegemony of Islamists at the national level and its communist commitment generated insecurity for US hegemony at the global level. The national response to the presence of Soviet troops in Afghanistan was more or less reactionary. The anti-secular Islamic forces strongly reacted against the 'infidelity' of the Soviet-backed Leftist government of Afghanistan. Claude Bruderlein writes:

> In the face of the Soviet invasion, both the rural population and
> sectors of disenchanted urban technocrats rallied around the

---

globalisation order. See Cox, 2001, op.cit, p. 48.

[225] Marx, Karl 1852 *The Eighteenth Brumaire of Louis Bonaparte*, available at http://www.marxists.org/archive/marx/works/1852/18th-brumaire/ch01.htm

[226] Gill, Stephen 1993 'Epistemology, Ontology and the "Italian School"' in Gill, Stephen (ed.) *Gramsci, Historical Materialism and International Relations*, Cambridge University Press, p.23.

call for jihad or a religious war, similar to those which had been evoked in response to earlier colonial invasions...Secularism was portrayed as the hidden goal of the Leftist intellectuals in power. The emancipation of women, used by the Communist authorities as a key objective of social reforms, was particularly perceived as an occupation ideology. In many rural areas, the emancipated Afghan women were referred to as 'the Russians'. In response to this, a new group of Islamists emerged who resented the reformist agenda of the Left which was seen as a foreign inspiration.[227]

These Islamists gave birth to the Mujahideen movement which mobilised the rural and urban Afghan social forces against the secular and foreign-controlled Leftist government of Afghanistan.

The Soviet presence not only jolted the national political climate of Afghanistan, but also proved to be an alarming development in global politics, especially in the suspicious political atmosphere unleashed by the Cold War. The US viewed the Soviet invasion as an expansionist gesture of communism which could adversely affect the prospect for a world order based on capitalist hegemony. In its attempt to counter the Soviet influence in Afghanistan, the US began to support the Islamists, or the Mujahideen, who had already been organising themselves against the Soviet-backed Leftist regime. This was a historical moment characterised by the temporary coalition of two diverse hegemonic social forces in Afghanistan: First, the Mujahideen made up of seven distinct political organisations mostly dominated by ethnic Pashtuns who had hegemonised Afghanistan since its inception as a modern nation-state in 1747; second, the Americans who had hegemonised the world since the end of the Second World War in 1945. The coalition of these national and global hegemonic forces prevailed during the Cold War when both pursued the common anti-Soviet strategy, albeit for different reasons – the Mujahideen for their anti-infidel stand and the Americans for their anti-communist orientation.

Contradictions in this hegemonic coalition appeared when Soviet forces were withdrawn from Afghanistan and the Cold War came to an end. Since the national and global hegemonic forces no longer shared the common objective of ousting the Soviet troops, their respective hegemonic strategies no longer coalesced. While the collapse of the Soviet Union reduced the importance of Afghanistan as a venue for furthering US hegemonic goals, it deprived the Mujahideen of their common enemy. In the absence of a common enemy, the

[227] Bruderlein, Claude (et. al.) 2002 'The Role of Islam in Shaping the Future of Afghanistan', *Peace Initiatives*, Vol. 8, Nos. 1-3, p.49.

Pashtun-dominated political organisations of the Mujahideen became separated, thereby causing a split in the national hegemony of Pashtuns. In the words of Amin Saikal:

> While the multiplicity of organizations during the war against the Soviets enabled the Pashtuns to receive more than their fair share of foreign military and financial aid, it also promoted rivalry, suspicion, and frequently violent clashes between them. This intra-Pashtun conflict prevented the leaders of Pashtun-dominated organizations to take a united political stand during the chaotic downfall of the communist regime.[228]

The split in national hegemony created space for several fragmented counter-hegemonic struggles wherein different non-Pashtun ethnic groups began to make separate efforts to challenge the traditional Pashtun hegemony in Afghan politics. Dilip Hiro writes:

> With the common enemy finally gone for good, long-standing rivalries between four major ethnic groups re-emerged. Having enjoyed autonomy, stemming from access to large quantities of weapons and money, in their decade-long struggle against the Leftist regime, the non-Pashtun minorities were not prepared to let the Pashtun hegemony, stretching back to 1747, re-assert itself. With Kabul now controlled by Tajik, Uzbek and Hazara fighters, and with the Defense Ministry run by Massoud [a Tajik], the ethnic minorities were in a strong position to frustrate Pashtuns' attempt to become the ruling group – as was the intent of Hizb-e-Islami's Hikmatyar.[229]

While the ethnic rivalry for establishing national hegemony in Afghanistan remained inconclusive, the US distanced itself from Afghanistan's domestic affairs and relished its unchallenged global hegemony after the collapse of the Soviet Union.

The lack of unity between non-Pashtun ethnic minorities prevented them from effectively challenging the Pashtun hegemony in Afghanistan. The fragmented nature of anti-Pashtun counter-hegemonic struggle can be attributed to the absence of an alternative knowledge-base which could

---

[228] Saikal, Amin 2006 *Modern Afghanistan: A History of Struggle and Survival*, I. B. Tauris, p.210. For an authoritative account of Afghan-Pashtun nation see Elphinstone, Mountstuart 1972 *An Account of the Kingdom of Caubul*, Vol.1, Oxford University Press.
[229] Hiro, Dilip 2002 *War Without End: The Rise of Islamist Terrorism and Global Response,* Routledge, p.233.

potentially bind the non-Pashtuns together in new social relations of production. While the non-Pashtuns failed to provide an agenda for generating an alternative knowledge-base and the corresponding social relations of production, the Pashtuns, now reorganised under the aegis of the Taliban and al-Qaida, evoked 'Sharia' as the alternative source of knowledge. The Taliban and al-Qaida began to run madrassas that focused on the teaching of a strictly puritanical Islam based on the orthodox and medievalist interpretations of the Deobandi and Wahhabi Islamic schools. Claiming to be informed by the religious maxims of Islam, the Taliban and al-Qaida called for establishing peace through restoring pre-modern social relations.

On 28 September 1996, a day after the Taliban came to power, Radio Shariat – the renamed Radio Kabul - broadcast the following decrees in accordance with Sharia:

> Any person with firearm must deposit it at a military post or the nearest mosque. Girls and women are not allowed to work outside home. All women who have to leave their homes must be accompanied by a *mahrim* (male blood relative). Public transport will be segregated, with separate buses for men and women. Men must grow beards and wear a turban or white beret. Suits and ties are forbidden... Women and girls must wear the burqa.[230]

The decrees issued in the following days prohibited women from visiting a male doctor or a male tailor. A young woman must not converse with a young man. Muslim families were forbidden to take photos or make videos. They could not listen to music. No merchant could sell alcohol or women's clothes.

Apart from introducing changes in the social sphere, the Taliban also brought about a drastic transformation in the Afghan economy. The localised predatory warlordism of the pre-Taliban era was replaced with a weak kind of rentier state power based on a criminalised open economy. Commenting on the transformed social relations of production during Taliban rule, Barnett R. Rubin writes:

> The replacement of the khan-dominated subsistence and local-trade economy by a warlord-dominated commercial agriculture tied to long-distance contraband provided the

---

[230] Ibid, p.250.

newly armed elite [the Taliban] with the opportunity to mobilise resources to exercise power directly, as it never did before.[231]

The new social relations of production promoted by the Taliban and al-Qaida were in many ways an attempt to move backwards in history. The Taliban and al-Qaida believed that turning the clock backwards would not only lift Afghanistan from the abyss of civil war but also combat the anti-Islamic forces operating at the global level, thereby paving the way for global Islamic hegemony. Amin Saikal writes:

> Initially, the Taliban leaders announced that their desire was to bring peace to Afghanistan by disposing of all Mujahideen factions. But as the militia's territorial control expanded, its political-ideological agenda made it explicit that their ultimate goal was to transform Afghanistan into a pure Islamic Emirate as a prelude to achieving wider regional objectives.[232]

The wider objectives included waging jihad for liberating Muslim lands from the control of infidels and uniting all Muslims within a single community or 'ummah'. The Afghans chose to accept the alternative offered by the Taliban and al-Qaida, even if it meant reaffirming the Pashtun hegemony in Afghan politics, in their desperation to come out of the difficult situations created by civil war. Whereas, the US provided humanitarian assistance to the Taliban regime as its policy towards Afghanistan had shifted back to its more traditional posture of benign neglect.[233] The US State Department spokesman, Glyn Davies, said there was 'nothing objectionable' about the domestic policies pursued by the Taliban.[234] While the domestic policies of the Taliban did not pose any direct threat to US hegemony in global politics, its increasingly aggressive and ambitious foreign policy certainly did.

The US ambassador Michael Sheehan stated:

> The Taliban provides safe haven for Osama bin Laden and his network. Because of the room, which the Taliban gives him to operate, bin Laden has created a truly transnational terrorist

---

[231] Rubin, Barnett R. 1999 'The Political Economy of War and Peace in Afghanistan' available at http://citeseerx.ist.psu.edu/viewdoc/
download?doi=10.1.1.461.517&rep=rep1&type=pdf
[232] Saikal, Amin 2006, op.cit, p.222.
[233] Lansford, Tom and Covarrubias 2003 'Osama bin Laden, Radical Islam and the United States' in Hayden, Patrick (et.al) (eds.) *America's War on Terror*, Ashgate, p.13.
[234] Goodarzi, Jubin November 13, 1996 'Washington and the Taliban', *Green Left Weekly* available at http://www.greenleft.org.au/node/13052

enterprise, drawing on recruits from across Asia, Africa, and Europe, as well as the Middle East. The Taliban has also given logistic support to members of other terrorist organizations, such as the Egyptian Islamic Jihad, the Algerian Armed Islamic Group, Kashmiri separatists, and a number of militant organizations from Central Asia...The ability of groups [such as al-Qaida] to plan and carry out terrorist attacks with impunity brings us to the final causal factor in the shift of terrorism to South Asia – the Taliban's refusal to crackdown on terrorists...(the) threat posed by bin Laden illustrates the challenges we face as non-state terrorism becomes more prevalent.[235]

The US, that initially had no objection to the rise of Pashtun hegemony under the leadership of the Taliban and al-Qaida, gradually became critical of it as its violent tendencies were no longer restricted to the frontiers of Afghanistan, but had started affecting the global peace.

The terrorist attacks of 9/11 added fuel to this long-standing anguish of the US and the declaration of war on terror in Afghanistan was its explosive consequence. This was a unique historical juncture that witnessed a direct confrontation between the same national and global hegemonic forces that had once formed a temporary coalition in Afghanistan. Now their hegemonic aspirations clashed with each other. In this clash of hegemonic aspirations, the US and the Taliban/al-Qaida produced their own versions of the dominant form of knowledge. Within the US, sources propagated the clash of civilizations doctrine to breed support for the government's global war on terror, while the Taliban/al-Qaida disseminated a similar Jihadist ideology to generate consent for their ideal of ummah. Huntington's clash of civilizations thesis has been hotly debated and al-Qaida's *Knights Under the Prophet's Banner* and *Military Studies in the Jihad against the Tyrants* have been widely read and religiously followed. Though these hegemonic discourses continue to grasp the psyche of a large section of people across the globe, their gradually weakening influence becomes apparent in the increasing use of force by both the US and the Taliban/al-Qaida.

Between the growing coercive force and diminishing consensual basis of these hegemonic aspirants lie the fraudulent ties between the US-led coalition force, the Karzai government, and the Taliban warlords.[236] The deep-

---

[235] Ambassador Michael Sheehan, 12 July, 2000 Office of the Coordinator for Counter Terrorism, Testimony Before the House International Relations Committee, Washington, DC.
[236] Chatterjee, Pratap 2010 'Paying Off the Warlords: Anatomy of a Culture of

rooted corruption in post-9/11 Afghan politics has not only created confusion but has also generated apathy in Afghan civil society. Though there are some progressive elements – political organisations like RAWA (Revolutionary Association of Women of Afghanistan) and Afghanistan Solidarity Party, the NGOs like the Humanitarian Assistance for Women and Children of Afghanistan (HAWCA) and Afghanistan Child Education and Care Organization (AFCECO) – that are working to curb political corruption and uplift the status of the Afghans, their uncoordinated and at times hidden efforts are barely organised around a supporting alternative knowledge-base or social relations of production. These efforts are therefore hardly sufficient to take the shape of any effective counter-hegemonic struggle. For estimating the future potential of these progressive elements in transforming the post-9/11 Afghan crisis, it is important to know whether the Afghan speech community has been historically open to, and accommodative of, the excluded progressive voices, and whether the dialogic tensions produced by the constructive expression of these voices have been successful in strengthening the counter-hegemonic struggle in Afghanistan.

Locating the Dialogic Tensions

Ernest Laclau and Chantal Mouffe note that 'the material reproduction of society is part of the *discursive* totalities which determine the meaning of the most sublime forms of political and intellectual life (an activity which is central to retaining hegemony)'.[237] If discursion is important for retaining hegemony, it is equally crucial for countering hegemony. The formation of counter-hegemony is largely a discursive and dialogic exercise which involves demands from bottom-up forces for inclusive deliberation, rational argument, inter-subjective agreement and bargained compromise. Andrew Linklater seeks to make clear that dialogue and consent replace domination and force as the central causal mechanisms in international relations.[238] He explains how the critical-theoretical enterprise continues to evolve beyond the production paradigm to a commitment to dialogic communities that are sensitive about all forms of inclusion and exclusion – domestic, transnational, and international.[239]

Corruption' and Roston, Aram 2010 'How the US Funds the Taliban' in Turse, op.cit, pp. 81-95.

[237] Laclau, Ernest and Mouffe Chantal 1987 'Post-Marxism without Apologies', *New Left Review* available at http://sites.google.com/site/sgboehm/laclau-mouffe-nlr.pdf.

[238] Payne, Rodger A. 2000 'Habermas, Discourse Norms, and the Prospects for Global Deliberation', a paper presented at the 41st Annual Convention of International Studies Association, Los Angeles, California.

[239] Linklater, Andrew 2001 'The Changing Contours of Critical International Relations Theory' in Jones, Richard Wyn (ed.), op.cit, p.25.

Describing the features of an 'authentic' dialogic exercise, Habermas writes:

> The procedures essential to authentic dialogue include the convention that no person and no moral position can be excluded from dialogue in advance, there is no priori certainty about who will learn from whom and when all are willing to engage in a process of reciprocal critique as a result...What guides participants is a commitment to be moved simply by the force of the better argument'.[240]

Inspired by this Habermasian discourse ethics, Linklater argues that an authentic dialogue aims at 'removing the modes of exclusion which obstruct the goal – which may never be realised – of global arrangements which rest upon the consent of each and every member of the human race.'[241]

Linklater stresses the need to yoke the 'defence of dialogue' to a critique of asymmetries of wealth and power.[242] He believes that an authentic dialogic exercise can help to criticise the existing hegemonic structure, highlight its inherent contradictions, and formulate an alternative consensus. The 'common consciousness' aroused from this alternative consensus can eventually lead to the collapse of hegemony and the formation of counter-hegemony.[243] Linklater states:

> Dialogue is not confined to maximizing consensus within the normative parameters which dominant groups take for granted. One of its key purposes is to widen social parameters by making it possible for individuals to expand the realm of admissible disagreements which political communities have most often suppressed in the name of the totalizing project... What moral progress refers to is the widening of the circle of those who have rights to participate in dialogue and the commitment that norms cannot be regarded as universally valid unless they have, or could command, the consent of all those who stand to be affected by them. [244]

---

[240] Habermas, J. 1990 *Moral Consciousness and Communicative Action,* MIT Press, p. 26.

[241] Linklater, Andrew 1998 *The Transformation of Political Community: Ethical Foundations of the Post-Westphalian Era,* University of South Carolina Press, p.93.

[242] Jones, Richard Wyn (ed.), op.cit, p.18.

[243] See Laclau, Ernest and Mouffe, Chantal 1985 *Hegemony and Socialist Strategy: Towards a Radical Democratic Politics,* Verso, pp.192-193.

[244] Linklater, Andrew 1998, op.cit, p.96.

Linklater notes that overlooking and silencing the actors affected by a decision perpetuates hegemony. He laments that the contemporary international political order has a 'tenuous existence and precarious legitimacy'[245] because decisions are taken without considering their likely effects on systematically excluded groups. In order to rectify this injustice, the states which have contested various forms of exclusion within their boundaries must start questioning exclusion in international affairs. A 'good international citizenship' is about assisting the weak and vulnerable communities[246] by attempting to include their hitherto suppressed voices in the prevalent counter-hegemonic discourse. The questioning of exclusionary practices is integral to the counter-hegemonic struggle.

A successful counter-hegemonic struggle not only questions exclusion but also demands a sound 'consensual legitimacy'. In order to generate consensual legitimacy, Linklater suggests that the world community's members should develop and identify their shared views through deliberation. Linklater calls for the formation of an 'ideal speech community' which can serve as a mechanism of transformation and legitimisation in a post-Westphalian global political order.[247] The ideal speech community endorses the practice of an open dialogue not only between fellow citizens but, more radically, between all members of the human species.[248] Linklater writes:

> Critical theory judges social arrangements by their capacity to embrace open dialogue with all others and envisages new forms of political community which break with unjustified exclusion...Critical theory envisages the use of unconstrained discourse to determine the moral significance of national boundaries and to examine the post-sovereign forms of political life.[249]

Linklater does not present these views as a mere idealist caprice. He is aware that conducting an unconstrained discourse cannot be the panacea for

---

[245] Ibid, p.17.

[246] Linklater, Andrew 1992 'What is a Good International Citizen?' in Paul Keal (ed.) *Ethics and Foreign Policy*, Allen and Unwin, p. 21-43. For understanding the difference in the nature of obligations of 'men' and 'citizens' see Linklater, Andrew 1981 'Men and Citizens in International Relations', *Review of International Studies*, Vol.7, No. 10, pp.23-37.

[247] See Linklater, Andrew 2007 *Critical Theory and World Politics: Citizenship, Sovereignty and Humanity*, Routledge.

[248] Linklater, Andrew 1996 'The Achievements of Critical Theory' in Smith, S., Booth, K. and Zalewski, M. (eds.) *International Theory: Positivism and Beyond*, Cambridge University Press, p.296.

[249] Ibid, pp. 279-280.

all ills. He, however, appreciates the process of arriving at an 'understanding' (which may not culminate in a moral consensus) as a significant starting point in achieving the 'praxeological'[250] goals of CIT. The shared understandings obtained through an authentic global dialogue can underpin 'non-arbitrary' norms and policies which in turn might prove instrumental in practically resolving highly contested disputes amongst advocates of various normative orders.

Linklater's idea of global dialogue defends a strong cosmopolitan moral orientation coupled with radical institutional innovations. However, his idea of cosmopolitanism is not synonymous with solidarism or unity achieved through homogenisation. Cautioning against the evil of unilateralism masquerading as solidarism, Linklater writes: 'Where a requisite consensus fails to emerge, solidarists-at-heart should be resigned, perhaps temporarily, to take on a pluralist stance'.[251] Linklater's vision of cosmopolitanism calls for a 'genuine solidarism' that encourages the achievement of consensual legitimacy through contestation of plural viewpoints. The emancipatory effect of genuine solidarism permits CIT to contribute to the next stage of international relations theory.[252] The next stage envisaged by Linklater's theoretical enterprise revolves around three realms: normative, sociological and praxeological. The *normative realm* diagnoses the non-arbitrary principles that can be used to criticise the existing hegemony and to imagine a counter-hegemonic order. The *sociological* realm traces the historical development of these non-arbitrary principles in the society of states. The *praxeological* realm points out the accumulated 'moral capital'[253] that can be exploited for establishing new forms of political communities.

The supplementation of Linklater's three realms with the Coxian analysis can offer an interesting way of revealing the unexplored nexus between hegemonic shifts and dialogic tensions in post-9/11 Afghanistan. For understanding the hegemonic shifts in terms of dialogic tensions in post-9/11

---

[250] The term 'praxeology', which is concerned with the practical application of theoretical constructs, was introduced by Raymond Aron in the course of his reflections on the antinomies of statecraft. He asserted that the tension between Machiavellian calculations of opportunity and the Kantian problem of acting ethically is at the heart of foreign policy. See Aron, Raymond 1966 *Peace and War: A Theory of International Relations,* Weidenfeld and Nicholson, pp.577-579.

[251] See Linklater, Andrew and Suganami, Hidemi 2006 *The English School of International Relations: A Contemporary Reassessment,* Cambridge University Press, pp.270-272.

[252] Linklater, Andrew 1992 'The Question of the Next Stage in International Relations Theory', *Millennium*, Vol.21, No.1, pp77-98.

[253] See Brown, Christopher Leslie 2006 *Moral Capital: Foundations of British Abolitionism,* UNC Press Books, p.457.

Afghan politics, one needs to pose the following questions: First, on what normative grounds (non-arbitrary principles?) did the hegemonic discourses in post-9/11 Afghan history systematically include or exclude specific voices? Second, have the hitherto excluded voices been able to generate a 'moral capital' that could constitute the basis of a genuine counter-hegemonic struggle? These questions can be examined in the context of two clearly identifiable phases of Pashtun hegemony in recent Afghan history: The first hegemonic phase appeared when the Pashtun-dominated Mujahideen joined hands to fight against the Soviets. The second hegemonic phase emerged when the Pashtuns, reorganised under the Taliban, and al-Qaida came together to fight against the Americans.

During the first hegemonic phase, the hegemonic discourse produced by the Mujahideen promoted two norms: pro-Islam and anti-foreign.[254] The Afghans, who had always been fiercely religious and independent,[255] supported these norms. The norms especially provided relief to those Afghans who felt betrayed by the reformism and secularism of the leaders of Soviet-backed People's Democratic Party of Afghanistan (PDPA). When the then President Taraki declared: 'We want to clean Islam in Afghanistan of the ballast and dirt of bad traditions, superstition and erroneous belief',[256] the overwhelming majority of Afghan society turned against the PDPA regime. The statement of Taraki was considered as an attack on the traditional Afghan way of life. Louis Dupree reported:

> [The Afghans held that] the PDPA policies violated practically every Afghan cultural norm, and strayed far beyond the allowable bounds of deviance in the social, economic, and political institutions. It appeared that they systematically planned to alienate every segment of the Afghan people.[257]

The Mujahideen, who raised their voice against the anti-Islamism of the Soviet-backed PDPA regime, quickly captured the grievance of almost all segments of Afghan people. The Afghans immediately responded to the 'fatwa' (a religious opinion concerning Islamic Law) issued by the Mujahideen leader Sheikh Abdullah Azzam – *Defense of the Muslim Lands, the First Obligation after Faith* – wherein it was stated that both the Afghan and

---

[254] Jalali, Ali Ahmad 2002 *Afghan Guerrilla Warfare: In the Words of the Mujahideen Fighters,* Zenith Press.

[255] Garthoff, Raymond L. 1994 *Detente and Confrontation: American-Soviet Relations from Nixon to Reagan,* Brookings Institution Press, p. 990.

[256] Hayden, Patrick, op.cit, p.7.

[257] Dupree, Louis 1980 'Red Flag over the Hindu Kush pt.3: Rhetoric and Reforms, or Promises! Promises!' *American Universities Field Staff Report* 23, p.4.

Palestinian struggles were jihads in which killing occupiers of one's land (no matter what their faith) was 'fard ayn' (a personal obligation) *for all Muslims.* Azzam declared:

> The Islamists have been the first to take control of the battles in Afghanistan. Those who lead the jihad in Afghanistan are the sons of the Islamic movement, the Ulama and Hafiz of Qur'an… While, in Palestine the [Islamic] leadership has been appropriated by a variety of people, of them *sincere Muslims*, communists, nationalists and modernists Muslims…the situation in Afghanistan is still in the hands of the Mujahideen. They continue to refuse help from any kafir country…There are more than 3000 kilometres of open border in Afghanistan and regions of tribes not under political influence. This forms a protective shield for Mujahideen.[258]

A close reading of this fatwa reveals that the Mujahideen discourse was exclusionary in two ways: First, though it intended to include all the Muslims, it preferred the 'sincere Muslims' who were not modernists and not under any other non-Islamic political influence. Second, it rejected the possibility of an open dialogue with non-Muslims as they were considered as kafirs. 'Jihad and the rifle alone…No negotiations, No conferences and *No dialogue*', was the slogan given by Azzam.[259] The repercussions of this exclusionary attitude became visible at two levels. At the national level, the Muslim sentiment present in the Mujahideen discourse temporarily mobilised all the ethnic groups of Afghanistan against the Soviets, but its 'selective' Islamic preference resulted in the formation of a loose Islamic Alliance which soon collapsed after the withdrawal of the Soviet troops from Afghanistan.

At the global level, the principle of non-engagement with non-Muslims was not translated into actual practice by the Mujahideen. Despite the closed nature of the Mujahideen discourse, the Mujahideen movement sought external support not just from Islamic states such as Iran, Saudi Arabia, and Pakistan, but also from the US which was supposed to be treated as a kafir country as per the standards of the Mujahideen. In fact, the Mujahideen

---

[258] Azzam, Sheikh Abdullah 'Defence of the Muslim Lands: The First Obligation after Iman' available at http://www.religioscope.com/info/doc/jihad/azzam_defence_1_table. htm

[259] Azzam, Sheikh Abdullah *The Lofty Mountain, Azzam Publications.* For a detailed study on Azzam's leading role in promoting and developing the modern Islamist concept of jihad, see McGregor, Andrew 2003 'Jihad and the Rifle Alone: Abdullah Azzam and the Islamist Revolution', *The Journal of Conflict Studies*, Vol 23, No. 2 available at https://journals.lib.unb.ca/index.php/jcs/article/view/219/377

sought to set one hegemonic aspirant against the other at the global level in order to retain the Islamic hegemony at the national level. However, the gap between the verbal declarations and practical strategy of the Mujahideen proved disastrous. The ethnic rivalry for receiving military and financial aid from diverse external sources caused feuding not only amongst the Pashtun-dominated organisations of the Mujahideen, but also amongst the various Afghan ethnicities. This rivalry ultimately led to the fall of Pashtun hegemony and caused a civil war in Afghanistan.

After four years of bloody civil war, the Pashtuns began to reclaim their lost hegemonic status by launching the Taliban movement in a close alliance with al-Qaida. In this second phase of Pashtun hegemony, the hegemonic discourse generated by the Taliban/al-Qaida endorsed two norms: pro-martyrdom and anti-America. Though these norms reiterated the age-old sympathy for Islam and hatred for foreigners, the thrust this time was much more extreme and specific. The discourse directed the Afghans not only to kill but also to die in the name of Islam; and this killing and dying had the objective of destroying a single country – America. A similar sentiment was expressed by the Taliban leader, Mullah Omar, who stated:

> The current situation in Afghanistan is related to a bigger cause…that is the destruction of America…This is not a matter of weapons. We are hopeful for God's help. The real matter is the extinction of America. And, God willing, it [America] will fall to the ground…We will not accept a government of wrong-doers. We prefer death than to be a part of an evil government.[260]

The call for the destruction of America was combined with a guarantee of peace. The Afghans, who were fed up with the prolonged civil war, longed for peace and the Taliban/al-Qaida discourse held the promise to grant exactly that – via jihad against America. It was suggested that the jihad was bound to deliver peace, if not in this life, then in the afterlife. Assuring peace to the would-be martyrs in the fight against America, Osama bin Laden said: 'In our religion, there is a special place in the hereafter for those who participate in jihad'.[261] The road to peace went through jihad which essentially demanded blood, not words. Bin Laden made his intention clear to the Americans: 'Just like you kill us, we will kill you[262]… There is *no dialogue* except with weapons'.[263]

---

[260] 'Interview with Mullah Omar', op.cit.
[261] *Time magazine* May 6, 1996.
[262] *Al-Jazeera*, November 12, 2002.
[263] *Al-Jazeera*, October 18, 2003.

The Taliban/al-Qaida discourse clearly indicated a rupture in the dialogic possibilities between the Islamists and the Americans. This rupture meant the exclusion of Americans from the Afghan dialogic community. However, the Americans were not the sole category to be excluded. The emphasis on the hardened Islamic identity and the hatred for the 'kufr' in Taliban/al-Qaida discourse signalled an exclusionary intent that went beyond the Americans. At the global level, the Taliban and al-Qaida tended to exclude the voices of those secular Muslims who lived in the West. Aijaz Ahmad pointed out that the 'great number of secular individuals of Muslim extractions within Western countries who do not adopt Islamic identity [as per the dictates of the Islamists like the Taliban] ... get sidelined and occluded'.[264] At the national level, the Taliban/al-Qaida demonstrated exclusionary tendencies towards the Shia Hazaras. Maulawi Mohammed Hanif, a Taliban commander, announced to a crowd of 300 people summoned to a mosque that the policy of the Taliban was to 'exterminate' the Hazaras. Mullah Manon Niazi, the Taliban governor of Mazar-e-Sharif, made speeches at mosques and on radio inciting hatred of Hazaras. He said: 'Wherever you go we will catch you. If you go up, we will pull you down by your feet; if you hide below we will pull you up by your hair'.[265]

The excesses committed during the Taliban regime attracted criticism from all corners of the world. Despite the growing worldwide criticism, the Taliban/al-Qaida continued to spread destruction and to push their hegemonic discourse. Proudly taking responsibility for the terrorist attacks of 9/11, the al-Qaida leader, Osama bin Laden, commented:

> As I was looking at those towers that were destroyed in Lebanon, it occurred to me that we have to punish the transgressor with the same, and that we had to destroy the towers in America, so that they taste what we tasted and they stop killing our women and children.[266]

When bin Laden's pride in killing Americans was not shared by many religious leaders in Islamic societies and his terrorist acts were condemned as being un-Islamic,[267] he attempted to soften his tone:

---

[264]   Ahmad, Aijaz 2008 'Islam, Islamisms and the West', *Socialist Register,* p.12.

[265]   Sheridan, Michael November 1, 1998 'How the Taliban Slaughtered Thousands of People', *The Sunday Times* available at http://www.rawa.org/times.htm

[266]   'Bin Laden: Your Security is in Your Own hands', CNN World available at http://articles.cnn.com/2004-10-29/world/bin.laden.transcript_1_lebanon-george-w-bush-arab?_s=PM:WORLD

[267]   Acharya, Amitav 'Clash of Civilizations? No, of National Interests and Principles' available at http://www.cpdsindia.org/clashofcivilizations.htm

> I have already said that I am not involved in the 11 September attacks in the United States. As a Muslim, I try my best to avoid telling a lie. Neither I had any knowledge of these attacks nor do I consider the killing of innocent women, children, and other humans as an appreciable act. Islam strictly forbids causing harm to innocent women, children, and other people. Such a practice is forbidden even in the course of a battle...I have already said that we are against the American system, not against its people, whereas in these attacks, the common American people have been killed.[268]

After 9/11, though, bin Laden asserted that he was against the 'American system' and not against the 'American people', in the late 1990s he had fully supported the idea of killing American civilians. While speaking to ABC News in 1998, he stated: 'In today's wars, there are no morals. We do not have to differentiate between military or civilian. As far as we are concerned, they [Americans] are *all* targets'.[269] However, his statements made in response to this event clearly contradicted his previous utterances, thereby disseminating distorted meanings in the Afghan dialogic community.

The dialogic distortions created by the Taliban/al-Qaida seriously undermined their consensual legitimacy. The sudden undermining of consensual legitimacy resulted in greatly weakening their hegemony. Consequently, post-9/11 Afghan politics totally discarded the voice of the Taliban and took notice of only those anti-Taliban voices that had organised themselves under the aegis of the US-backed Northern Alliance. However, after the passage of more than a decade since 9/11, the leaders of the Northern Alliance seem to have shifted their attitude towards the Taliban.

The remarkable distancing of the Northern Alliance from the Taliban/al-Qaida, which guided the initial years of post-9/11 Afghan politics, has been replaced with the rise of a twofold trend in recent times: First, there has been a renewal in the ties between the Northern Alliance and the Taliban. US President Barack Obama encouraged the Northern Alliance to develop a certain closeness with the Taliban. He stated: 'We will support efforts by the [Northern Alliance] Afghan government to open the door to those Taliban who abandon violence and respect the human rights and their fellow citizens'.[270] Such Taliban have been labelled as 'good Taliban'. The discourse on

---

[268] Interview with *Karachi Ummat,* September 28, 2001.

[269] 'The Most Wanted Man in the World', September 16, 2001 *Time Magazine Profile* available at http://www.time.com/time/magazine/0,9263,7601010924,00.html

[270] Bennis, Phyllis 2009 'President Obama's Afghanistan Escalation Speech: An Assessment' available at https://www.tni.org/es/node/13231

distinguishing between 'good Taliban' and 'bad Taliban' aims at peeling off the reconcilable Taliban leaders from the irreconcilable ones[271]. The recent willingness of the American and Afghan officials to drop the names of 'good Taliban' from the UN blacklist of terrorists[272] further testifies to the growing intimacy between the Northern Alliance and the Taliban. Second, there has been a growing gulf in relations between the Taliban and al-Qaida. The Taliban publicly distanced itself from al-Qaida by releasing a statement that they would provide a 'legal guarantee' that they would not intervene in foreign countries if international troops withdraw from Afghanistan.[273] This statement caused a flurry of dissent from al-Qaida-linked militants, who posted sharply critical statements on several Islamic-extremist web sites. The latter declared a global jihad and rejected any collaboration with what were seen to be enemy governments, thereby signalling a parting of the ways with the Taliban.

The confusing shifts in allegiances have had the effect of obscuring the Afghan dialogic space. After witnessing frequent switches in allegiances during decades of war, many Afghans have stopped listening or speaking with confidence. A good number of Afghans are wary of the 'Taliban-appeasing policy' of the US-backed Northern Alliance, but they fear freely voicing their disapproval in the Afghan dialogic community. Though the critical voices of Afghan NGOs, INGOs, inter-governmental organisations, academic institutions, and donor governments have made an impressive entry in the Afghan dialogic community, they fail to generate a unified discourse. In the absence of a unified discourse, the anti-hegemonic moral capital remains under-exploited. The anti-hegemonic moral capital has been partially channelled by scattered critical voices, thereby creating a necessary but insufficient condition for forming an effective counter-hegemonic struggle. Post-9/11 Afghanistan stands at a crossroads marked by complex interactions between feeble hegemonic, as well as counter-hegemonic, social forces. The insights drawn from the dual paradigms of CIT can shed some light on its probable future direction.

The Way Ahead: Towards a Critical Solution to the 'Civilizational' Problem

The alternative vision derived from the vantage point of CIT deconstructs the

---

[271] Rubin, Trudy February 19, 2009 'Taming the Good Taliban' available at http://www. realclearworld.com/articles/2009/02/taming_the_good_taliban_afpak.html

[272] Filkins, Dexter Jan 24, 2010, 'U.N. Seeks to Drop Some Taliban From Terror List', *The New York Times* available at http://www.nytimes.com/2010/01/25/world/ asia/25taliban.html

[273] Gopal, Anand December 7, 2009 'Taliban Seek Deal on Foreign Forays', *The Wall Street Journal* available at http://online.wsj.com/article/SB126002422466878409.html

image of post-9/11 Afghanistan as a venue for clashing civilizations. Rather than being a case of civilizational clash, the post-9/11 Afghan scenario gets transformed into a classic instance of clashing hegemonic aspirations. Any exit from this troubling state of affairs requires the organisation of an effective counter-hegemonic struggle against both the national Pashtun hegemony and the global US hegemony. According to the lessons drawn from the dual paradigms of CIT, a significant step in this direction could be taken by accomplishing two tasks: First, designing an *alternative knowledge-base* that not only forms a critique of the prevailing hegemonic forces, but also organises the critical forces along *alternative social relations of production*. Second, creating an *all-inclusive speech community* that not only weaves the existing critical voices into a unified counter-hegemonic discourse but also puts forth the demand for inclusion of hitherto excluded voices – the voices of secular Muslims, Afghan women, non-Pashtun ethnicities (especially the Hazara), and the remaining progressive elements of Afghan civil society. Since the ideal speech community calls for an open dialogue not only between fellow citizens but also between all members of the human species, especially those who stand to be affected by the collective decisions taken through an open dialogue, the dialogic community in Afghanistan must include the voices of the non-Afghan stakeholders. However, the inclusion of non-Afghan voices by no means implies the imposition of foreign decisions on Afghan politics. The objective of forming an all-inclusive speech community is to enhance the 'rational' and 'consensual' components of those collective decisions that are to guide the future course of Afghan politics.

What could be the source of an alternative knowledge-base in Afghanistan? And how could it serve as a stepping stone in creating an all-inclusive Afghan speech community? Since the Quran – the founding document and scripture of Islam – has historically commanded the deepest influence and widest appeal in Afghanistan, it should be evoked in the process of formulating an alternative knowledge-base. However, the Quranic traits of the alternative knowledge-base must challenge the obscurantist interpretation of Islam propagated by orthodox Pashtuns and popularised by the US media. This can be done by presenting the Quran as a broad philosophical tradition rather than a narrow religious doctrine. Shabbir Akhtar writes:

> An important intellectual deficit in the modern house of Islam is the lack of a living philosophical culture that could influence its narrow religious outlook…The Quranic hermeneutics should not simply be a close domestic attention to the text aimed solely at extracting what is useful to believers…the Quran is intended to be revelation addressed to humankind, not merely a fixed body of laws and morals…Muslims should be alert to inter-faith reservations about their scripture…Without the

> spiritual introspection that philosophical insight brings, religion is no more than ritual...Muslim civilization would be enriched by the revival of a certain type of philosophy which could supplement the Quran's ancient religious and spiritual confidences.[274]

The critical social forces of Afghanistan must revive the philosophical underpinnings of the Quran while designing an alternative knowledge-base.

The adherence to such an Islamic philosophy would not only provide a check on the hubris of religious power, but also lay the foundation for an all-inclusive Afghan dialogic community. The philosophical approach to Quran would advocate 'inter-faith' discussions on Islam, thereby also creating ample space for a passionate dialogue between followers of religious, spiritual, and secular Islamic traditions. An open dialogue between various Islamic and non-Islamic voices would differently inform the common consciousness of the Afghans. The common consciousness raised by the cross-fertilisation of varied Islamic interpretations would transcend that concept of Islamism which sees it as an exclusivist and totalising ideology, thereby promoting a 'post-Islamic'[275] current that would espouse inclusion and pluralism. According to Asef Bayat, 'post-Islamism is not anti-Islamic or secular; a post-Islamist movement dearly upholds religion but also highlights citizens' rights. It aspires to 'a pious society within a democratic state'[276] in which all Muslims and non-Muslims could enjoy access to certain basic rights.

As opposed to the Islamism that has been 'the political language not just of the marginalised but particularly of high-achieving middle classes who saw their dream of social equity and justice betrayed by the failure of both capitalist modernity and socialist utopia'[277], the post-Islamic ideology would develop itself as the language of those Muslims and non-Muslims who have been the victims of Islamic fundamentalism. The inward-looking orientation of post-Islamic ideology would not only highlight the deficits of capitalism and socialism but also expose the loopholes of Islamic orthodoxy. Discussing the failure of Islamic movements in uplifting economic conditions, Gilbert Achcar writes:

---

[274] Akhtar, Shabbir 2008 *The Quran and the Secular Mind: A Philosophy of Islam,* Routledge, pp. 1-3; 328.

[275] Bayat, Asef 2008 'Islamism and Empire: The Incongruous Nature of Islamist Anti-Imperialism', *Socialist Register,* p.38.

[276] See Bayat, Asef 2011 'The Post-Islamist Revolutions', *Foreign Affairs,* available at http://www.foreignaffairs.com/articles/67812/asef-bayat/the-post-islamist-revolutions

[277] Bayat, 2008, op.cit, p.41.

> All these [Islamic] movements are clothed in religion but they
> have their source in economic causes; and yet, even when
> they are victorious, they allow the old economic conditions to
> persist untouched. So the old situation remains unchanged
> and the collision [between different Islamic forces as well as
> between Islamic and non-Islamic forces] recurs periodically.[278]

The periodic recurrence of collisions generates a criminalised war economy
like the one that exists in post-9/11 Afghanistan. The criminalised war
economy has left the power holders as unaccountable to most Afghan people
as they were under previous regimes. Most of the population are left to fend
for themselves, in conditions of greater security, but without a development
agenda. The post-Islamic ideology must learn from these past mistakes and
call for the establishment of alternative social relations of production that are
capable of undercutting the recurrent pattern of war economy and disbursing
the reconstruction aid in such a way that builds reciprocity between state and
civil society.

Who are the potential propagators of post-Islamism in today's Afghanistan?
And how could post-Islamism help them in producing a unified counter-
hegemonic discourse and in establishing the alternative social relations of
production? The propagators of post-Islamism could be those Afghans who
are disillusioned by the corrupt political practices of both the Taliban and the
US-backed Northern Alliance. Many Afghans initially viewed the Northern
alliance as an alternative to the Taliban, but now they stand betrayed in the
light of the growing closeness between these two organisations. Daud
Razmak, the leader of the Afghan Solidarity Party, states that he never
contested the elections in post-9/11 Afghanistan because he believed that the
Northern Alliance would rectify the wrongs done during the Taliban regime. He
therefore supported the Northern Alliance government from the outside.

However, his beliefs were proved wrong and now his party aims at securing
the independence of Afghanistan, not only from foreigners, but also from the
mafias working inside and outside the Northern Alliance regime. Maduda
(name changed), an activist associated with RAWA, identifies the Northern
Alliance, Taliban, and foreign forces as three enemies of the Afghans. She
discloses that the present parliamentarians are the former Mujahideen
involved in a variety of criminal activities. She criticises the secret ties
between the US-backed Afghan government and the Afghan opium cultivators
which constitute the basis of the criminalised war economy. Bulqis Roshan, a
Senator from Farah province, comments that the people in power in

---

[278] Achcar, Gilbert 2008 'Religion and Politics Today from a Marxian Perspective',
Socialist Register, pp.70-71.

Afghanistan are the former criminals. Earlier they used to commit direct crimes against the Afghans and now with foreign support they indirectly harass the Afghans. These criminals divided the Afghans who were otherwise always united against foreigners.

Najla Ayubi, the Director of Asia Foundation in Kabul, condemns the Taliban for killing the Afghans and not the ISAF officials. Saifuddin Saihoon, a Professor at Kabul University, criticises the excessive dependence of the Afghan government as well as Afghan civil society on foreign funds. He ridicules the Afghan government for being 'injected against' the criticisms coming from the Afghan people. Abdul Latif Rasif, a judge at the Kabul Court, opines that 70 percent of the people of Afghanistan are against the Karzai government. He feels that the political strategy of the Karzai government is not very clear. The Karzai government forces itself on the judiciary in order to cover its corrupt political practices. The widespread political corruption is adversely affecting the activities of Afghan civil society. He says that the lawyers and judges of Afghanistan are organising themselves against the politically corrupt Karzai regime. Wahid Paikan, a BBC journalist in Kabul, holds that the people in Afghanistan might not be educated but they are experienced as they have long been attending the 'war university'. They do not see any progress and continue to live an insecure life. They are guided by an anti-Karzai sentiment and they want the foreign forces to leave.

Though diverse social forces in Afghanistan are critical of the corrupt political practices, their critical voices are not well organised. Andeisha Farid, the Director of AFCECO, an NGO that works for the welfare of the children of Afghanistan, points out that Afghan civil society has become a playground of many NGOs funded by foreign donors, not all of them are free from corruption. Even the corrupt government officials are running their own NGOs (the daughter of warlord Rashid Khan runs an NGO for women's empowerment in Herat.). Farid concludes that there is no unified civil society movement in Afghanistan.[279] Post-Islamism could potentially act as a philosophical adhesive for binding the fragmented critical voices of the Afghan dialogic community, thereby contributing towards the formation of a unified civil society movement backed by a unified counter-hegemonic discourse. The unified counter-hegemonic discourse could more effectively mobilise those critical social forces which are either apathetically silent or systematically excluded.

Post-Islamism presents a viable philosophical basis for an alternative

---

[279] The opinions of Razmak, Maduda, Roshan, Ayubi, Saihoon, Rasif, Paikan and Farid were expressed in a series of interviews conducted by the author during her visit to Kabul in July, 2011.

knowledge-base in Afghan politics. However, its potential to foster an alternative Afghan economy seems weak at least in the short-run. Given the complex and constantly shifting power nexus between various hegemonic forces in post-9/11 Afghanistan, the building of alternative social relations of production appears to be a herculean task. Nonetheless, a preliminary post-Islamic agenda for achieving this goal could draw inspiration from Michael Lowy's idea of 'elective affinity'. Lowy evoked the term 'elective affinity' to explain the Christian liberation theology that allowed Christianity to turn into the institutionalised ideology of communistic utopianism in Latin America.[280] Guided by the Latin American experiment of elective affinity, the critical social forces in post-9/11 Afghanistan must strive to construct a post-Islamic liberation theology that could permit Islam to breed such governmental institutions that could redress the grievances of the poor Afghans and genuinely work for transforming their miserable conditions of existence.

Contrasting the differential strategies adopted by the Islamists and the Christian liberation theologians, Asef Bayat writes:

> While Islamists aimed to Islamise their society, polity and economy, liberation theologians never intended to Christianise their society or states, but rather to change society from the vantage point of the deprived. Liberation theology, then, had much in common with humanist, democratic, and popular movements in Latin America, including labour unions, peasant leagues, student groups and guerrilla movements, with whom it organised campaigns, strikes, demonstrations, land occupation and development work.[281]

While the narrow religious outlook of Islamists in Afghanistan made them more interested in Islamising the Afghans and less interested in uplifting the backward economy of Afghanistan, the broad philosophical orientation of post-Islamists can help them in prioritising their goals in accordance with the needs of poor Afghans. Unlike the case of Latin America, Afghan civil society has not attained a higher level of cohesion and lacks well organised popular movements. However, the post-Islamists could make a beginning towards the establishment of pro-poor social relations of production by blending the tenets

---

[280] Lowy, Michael 1996 *The War of Gods: Religion and Politics in Latin America*, Verso. The concept of 'elective affinity' was initially applied by Max Weber to suggest a selective relationship between 'ideas' and 'interests'. See Howe, Richard Herbert 1978 'Max Weber's Elective Affinities: Sociology within the Bounds of Pure Reason', *American Journal of Sociology*, Vol. 84, No.2 available at http://www.jstor.org/ pss/2777853
[281] Bayat, 2008, op.cit, p. 48.

of Islam with the demands for banning opium cultivation, prohibiting the drugs and arms trade, developing crop-substitution mechanisms, finding alternative means of livelihood for opium farmers, devising alternative sources of income for landless labour, women, and returning refugees,[282] tracing alternative ways of financing Afghan state activities, decentralising the governance structures and incorporating the opinions of local shuras (councils) in the official process of planning and service provision, thereby placing poor Afghans at the centre of the production and re-production process. The marriage of post-Islamic ideology with pro-poor social relations of production in Afghanistan might appear to be a distant dream. However, the political agenda for realising this distant dream would not be incompatible with Quranic maxims. The ideas of struggle, charity, and emancipation are already enmeshed in the Quran which states:

> And what will explain to you what the steep path is? It is the freeing of a slave from bondage, or the giving of food in a day of famine to an orphan relative, or to a needy in distress. Then will he be of those who believe, enjoin fortitude and encourage kindness and compassion.[283]

The humanistic re-interpretation of Quranic verses by the post-Islamic counter-hegemonic forces in Afghanistan would not only aid in the transformation of the post-9/11 Afghan crisis, but would also vindicate Islam against its distortion and demonisation by both Muslim and non-Muslim hegemonic aspirants in the contemporary world.

---

[282] Siddharth Dev Burman, a UN bureaucrat posted in Kabul, pointed out in an interview with the author that contemporary Afghan society had no middle class as the Afghans belonging to the upper middle class have settled in Western countries while the Afghans belonging to the lower middle class have become refugees in Pakistan in the aftermath of the post-9/11 war on terror in Afghanistan.

[283] Quran, Chapter 90, Verses 12-17 available at http://www.religioustolerance.org/isl_qura.htm

6

Conclusion

The historic event of 9/11 reminded Brendan Simms of the words of poet William Butler Yeats: 'All changed, changed utterly - a terrible beauty is born'. Yeats was describing the transformation of Irish politics wrought by the seemingly hopeless Easter Rising of 1916 against British rule. These words resonated again on September 11, 2001 when a number of jihadists attempted to inflict damage on the informal American empire by attacking the World Trade Center and the Pentagon. What had changed after 9/11? And which terrible beauty was born in the wake of it? The 9/11 attacks symbolically challenged the hegemony of the world's sole superpower, reinforced the demonic image of Islam and provided a launching pad to an indefinite US-led global war on terror with Afghanistan as its starting point. The terrible beauty born out of these catastrophic developments was the 'popular acceptance' of a world laden with frequent devastating clashes between so-called terrorist and democratic forces. While the idea of eliminating terrorism and spreading democracy was beautiful, the permanent labelling of certain forces as 'terrorist' and the others as 'democratic' was terrible.

Against this circumstantial backdrop, the thesis of civilizational clash propagated by Huntington gained momentum. Huntington's thesis, which had projected a post-Cold War world marked by bloody conflicts between different civilizations, especially between the Western and Islamic civilizations, not only became instrumental in legitimising the US-led military operations in Afghanistan, but also in reaffirming a similar jihadist worldview endorsed by a few orthodox Islamists operating in Afghanistan. Was this civilizational approach to decode post-9/11 Afghan politics theoretically appropriate and, or, strategically prudent? This study began with the objective of providing a critical insight into the civilizational approach and offering an alternative understanding of post-9/11 Afghanistan. The attempt to fulfil this objective was carried out in four stages: (i) Designing a 'psychological critique' of the civilizational approach; (ii) Explaining the 'popular receptivity' of Huntington's civilizations thesis amongst the Afghans and demonstrating its harmful implications for post-9/11 Afghan politics; (iii) Establishing Critical

International Theory (CIT) as a more meritorious theoretical framework in comparison to Huntington's civilizations thesis; and (iv) Providing an alternative and more accurate vision of post-9/11 Afghan politics from the critical-theoretical standpoint.

Psychological Critique: The Knowledge-Violence Nexus

Critical insights into Huntington's civilizational approach had already been provided by scholars of diverse philosophical traditions. They have criticised the clash of civilizations thesis on epistemological, methodological, and ethical grounds. The epistemological critique condemned the clash of civilizations thesis based on its realist, orientalist and elitist outlook. The methodological critique attacked its *monolithic, inconsistent* and *reductionist/ essentialist* attitude while the ethical critique denounced it for being a *purposeful* thesis that fuelled enemy discourse and in the process, became a *self-fulfilling* prophecy. Though the critiques of Huntington's thesis strongly pointed out its various flaws, they were weaker when it came to explaining its receptivity not just amongst decision-makers and shapers but also amongst the masses across the globe. Despite the copious and essentially valid criticisms, the clash of civilizations thesis flourished. Any attempt to check this trend required a serious probing into the issue of how people became so receptive to such a provocative body of knowledge. In other words, how aggressive scripts like Huntington's thesis interacted with the psyche of the people so as to transform them into its violent agents? In an attempt to find an answer to this question, this study drew inspiration from the academic discipline of psychology. It evoked the humanistic-existential model of psychology for providing an explanation of the widespread receptivity of Huntington's thesis.

According to the humanistic-existential model, a combination of two paradoxical forces determined human behaviour. First, the *free agency* of the individual who was personally responsible for creating meanings in an apparently meaningless world; Second, the compulsion of the *conditions of existence* that influenced the individual's willingness or unwillingness to create or believe in a particular set of meanings. From this perspective, Huntington's thesis won receptivity because of two reasons: First, Huntington's willingness to generate a specific notion of reality; Second, the people's choice to identify their own perception of reality with that notion. In other words, Huntington's presentation of an imagined reality (i.e. false consciousness), which was defined in terms of a civilizational clash, became an actual reality (i.e. false real consciousness) only when people chose to believe in it and act or react upon it.

The purpose behind Huntington's decision to present reality in a specific way and the people's choice to accept it existed in their respective conditions of existence. Under the conditions of the post-Cold War world, the artificial construct of 'bloody Islamic borders' allowed Huntington to gain an influential position amongst the US foreign policymakers who were desperately looking for an alarming discourse which could justify their aggressive policies as legitimate defensive action. Huntington's deliberate ignorance of the miserable conditions of existence in Muslim societies and his attribution of their consequent frustration to a kind of civilizational-cultural-religious disorder assigned a new meaning to the persisting political issues. This new meaning served the purpose of its believers at many levels. Firstly, it helped US policymakers to divert the attention of both Muslims and non-Muslims away from the actual suffering and the creative possibilities of the Islamic world, thereby facilitating a guaranteed American hegemony. Secondly, it allowed the fundamentalists in both Islamic and Western societies to infuriate the masses, thereby paving the way for satisfying their personal ambitions.

Though Huntington's dangerous motive became obvious as soon as he activated his abstract idea of 'civilizational identity' by awakening a hatred for other civilizations, it was well-received by the people who found it helpful in their respective living conditions. The cascading effect of the abstract idea of 'civilizational identity' totally obscured the complexity of human identity formation, and thus weakened the effort at human emancipation. However, the humanistic-existential model was optimistic in its assertion that the popularity of Huntington's thesis was largely an outcome of the personal choice of human beings who were embedded in their respective conditions of existence as free agents. As such, the issue of acceptance or rejection of the civilizational approach became a matter of free choice and the responsibility for exposing its harmful implications rested on free individuals. In the light of the lessons drawn from this psychological critique, the study went further to uncover the psychological mechanism that granted political receptivity to Huntington's ideas in Afghanistan, thereby exposing its harmful impact on post-9/11 Afghan politics.

Political Receptivity: The Islamic Appeal for Pashtun Benefit

The study employed the combination of agency and structure, as stressed by the humanistic-existential model of psychology, for explaining the general history of political reception and the particular history of Huntington's reception in Afghan politics. A careful reading of Afghan history suggested that any political discourse was psychologically well received by the majority of Afghans if it possessed two features - first, the intellectual agency shaped the content of the discourse in such a way as to make a strong reference to

'Islam'; second, the intellectual structure, traditionally dominated by the ethnic Pashtuns (Tajiks, Uzbeks, Hazaras, and Nuristanis, being other less numerous Afghan ethnicities), found the discourse politically beneficial for itself. The awakening of Islamic content provides political benefits for Pashtuns since it potentially enables any political discourse incorporating the Islamic content to capture the 'social imaginary' of Afghans. Since the prevalence of Islam and the dominance of ethnic Pashtuns marked a historical continuity in Afghan politics, they remained crucial in determining the Afghan social imaginary. This study examined the receptivity or non-receptivity of the political discourses generated by different regimes in Afghanistan – Peoples' Democratic Party of Afghanistan (PDPA), the Mujahideen, the Taliban/al-Qaida – in terms of their success or failure to capture this Afghan social imaginary. The study then explained the popularity of Huntington's thesis amongst the Afghans by mapping its resemblance with the relatively more popular Taliban/al-Qaida discourse.

The study demonstrated that the Marxism-inspired and Soviet-backed PDPA discourse could not win ample support as it lacked Islamic content and held no promise for political benefit to the structurally dominant group of Pashtuns. The PDPA regime was followed by Mujahideen rule. In fact, the Mujahideen managed to enter the political mainstream by exposing the infidelity of the PDPA. In contrast to the attempted imposition of an atheistic Marxist regime by the PDPA, the Mujahideen claimed to establish an Islamic State of Afghanistan, thereby developing a religiously charged and therefore comparatively more effective political discourse. The Mujahideen discourse was rich in terms of both Islamic content and political attractiveness for ethnic Pashtuns. Six of the seven Mujahideen organisations were dominated by Pashtuns. However, the Mujahideen failed to deliver the promise of clear political benefit to Pashtuns as the non-Pashtun members refused to accept Pashtun dominance. Moreover, the Mujahideen coalition committed the mistake of excluding a major Pashtun organisation led by Gulbuddin Hikmatyar, thereby further causing division amongst the Pashtun majority. The moderate Islamism propagated by the Mujahideen discourse proved incapable of binding the Pashtuns together and was rapidly replaced with the Taliban's extremist medievalism in the name of Islam. The Taliban/al-Qaida discourse was more successful than the Mujahideen discourse. The study compared the 'contents' (the propounder's agency) and the 'attending circumstances' (the follower's structure) of these two discourses in order to explain the greater success of the Taliban/al-Qaida discourse.

A comparison of the contents of the Mujahideen and Taliban/al-Qaida discourses revealed the following points of departure. First, the Mujahideen discourse made an Islamic appeal to expel one country – the Soviet Union, whereas the Taliban/al-Qaida discourse activated the Islamic appeal primarily to destroy America, but also to attack all Western countries led by the US. Thus, the Taliban/al-Qaida discourse was meant to fight a larger and more powerful opposition. Second, the Mujahideen discourse presented the Soviets as infidels who had little respect for the believers of Islam, whereas the Taliban/al-Qaida discourse projected the Western countries not just as infidels but also as 'Zionist-Crusaders' who were the traditional enemies of the believers of Islam. Therefore, the Taliban/al-Qaida discourse was framed to deal with a more dangerous opposition that was not just disrespectful but also historically driven by the spirit of animosity against Islam. Third, the Mujahideen discourse sought to mobilise the diverse ethnic groups of Afghanistan, whereas the Taliban/al-Qaida discourse chiefly targeted the Pashtuns, not the other ethnic groups, as its potential audience. It contained a heavy dose of 'Pashtunwali' and reflected an 'anti-Shiite' inclination, thereby proving more successful in attracting the structurally dominant group of Pashtuns. Fourth, the Mujahideen discourse tried to channel the energy of Afghans against the Soviet-backed regime, whereas the Taliban/al-Qaida discourse aimed at raising all the Afghan and non-Afghan believers of Islam to fight for removing the Western interference from internal political affairs of all Muslim states in the world. The Taliban/al-Qaida discourse was more ambitious as it was designed to direct a transnational project.

The circumstantial factors attending the two discourses were compared at two levels – domestic and global. At the domestic level, the situation attending the Mujahideen discourse was marked by the weak political credentials of the Soviet-backed Najibullah regime, whereas the circumstances facing the arrival of the Taliban/al-Qaida discourse were defined by the eroded political legitimacy of mutually warring ethnicities of Mujahideen. In contrast to the Mujahideen discourse, the Taliban/al-Qaida discourse offered greater prospect for political benefit to ethnic Pashtuns as it promised the riddance of, and victory over, not just the foreign Soviet force, but also the domestic non-Pashtun forces comprising the warring factions of Mujahideen. The Taliban/al-Qaida discourse found a ready purchase amongst the Pashtuns also because it ignited the hope for resolving their age-old 'Pashtunistan issue', whereby they had been demanding an independent or semi-independent statehood for themselves. The study suggested that so long as the Taliban/al-Qaida discourse managed to keep the hope for concretising the dream of Pashtunistan alive, it was likely to retain its appeal amongst the majority of Afghans who are Pashtuns.

At the global level, the Mujahideen discourse emerged when the Soviet Union and its Stalinised model of governance was breaking up, whereas the Taliban/al-Qaida discourse originated when the US and its capitalist model of development was being declared as victorious. The comparatively weaker Soviet opponent of the Mujahideen discourse was not stimulating enough to bind the Afghans for long, whereas the hegemonic tendencies of the US continued to remain sufficiently challenging to provoke an ongoing protest by the Taliban and al-Qaida. Besides the provocations unleashed from the hegemonic tendencies of the US, the study attributed the resurgence of Islamic fundamentalism under the leadership of the Taliban and al-Qaida to the general decline of secular modernity. Against the backdrop of the poor performance of secular states, the alternative model of an 'Islamic state' offered by the Islamist movements easily gained widespread attention. It was no wonder that the extreme vision of Islamism propagated by the Taliban/al-Qaida discourse became immensely popular amongst the Afghans who were disillusioned by the efforts of various Afghan modernisers in uplifting their miserable living conditions.

The factors explaining the influential impact of the Taliban/al-Qaida discourse also provided clues for understanding the popularity of Huntington's thesis amongst the Afghans. The study traced a striking resemblance between the discourses generated by the Taliban/al-Qaida and Huntington. Like the Taliban/al-Qaida discourse, which established the West as the enemy of Islam and intended to mobilise Muslims around the world to safeguard their sacred Islamic lands from Western intervention, the Huntingtonian discourse of civilizational clash inversely matched these propositions by presenting Islam as the most intolerant and aggressive civilization that posed the greatest threat to the West. Huntington advised the West to protect itself from Islamic demons by exploiting the differences between the non-Western civilizations and by maintaining the superiority of the West. While the Taliban and al-Qaida appealed for Islamisation, Huntington called for Americanisation. Both the discourses emerged around the mid-1990s, uttered the language of religious war and fed upon their mutual enmity. The common violent thrusts of both the discourses continued to thrive upon their capacity to accept and reinforce each other. Huntington himself admitted this reality in an interview with Nathan Gardels. He stated that the terrorist actions of Osama bin Laden had reinvigorated civilizational identity. However, the study pointed out that the sense of common 'civilizational identity' had better served the interests of the US than that of the Afghans. The 'civilizational identity' had granted the US a profound ideological-political-diplomatic gain by enabling it to subordinate the UN and to create an 'international coalition' of states, many of which were themselves guilty of practicing terrorism. It had also allowed the US to have a military-political entry in Central Asia on a depth and scale that it never before had. By contrast, the activation of 'civilizational identity' by the Taliban and al-Qaida had not been able to deliver anything better than a war-torn, and insecure, nation for the Afghans.

The Afghans who believed in the Taliban/al-Qaida discourse were bound to succumb to the intellectual insights of Huntington's thesis which endorsed the same worldview in a reverse guise. The popularity of al-Zawahiri's text – *'Knights Under the Prophet's Banner'* – that presented a worldview comparable, but in reverse, to Huntington's thesis, confirmed this line of argument. The study asserted that the Afghans who were trapped in a vicious cycle generated by these two destructive discourses had not been able to bring an end to their tragic state of affairs and to tap their constructive potential for building an alternative theoretical and political discourse for themselves. It was suggested that the lack of an alternative theoretical-political discourse largely accounted for the absence of an alternative and peaceful way of life for the Afghans. In its search for an alternative discourse, the study examined the theoretical credentials of CIT, thereby highlighting its methodological edge over and above the clash of civilizations thesis.

The Meritorious Framework of CIT: Temporal and Spatial Sensitivity

For judging the relative merits of two or more substantive theories making competing claims about social reality, Rosenberg evoked Ian Craib's three criteria. First, the theory must be based on mutually *consistent* propositions. Second, the theory must be measured against *evidence*. Third, the theory must specify in *more detail* the causal processes at work and the situations in which the causal mechanisms come into operation. Judging by these criteria, the study attempted to establish CIT – that combined within its ambit two main sets of influences, the 'production paradigm' shaped by the work of Antonio Gramsci and introduced into IR by Robert Cox; and the 'communication paradigm' developed by the Frankfurt School (Habermas, Horkheimer, and Adorno) and applied to IR by Andrew Linklater – as a more meritorious theoretical framework than Huntington's clash of civilizations thesis. Before demonstrating the relative strengths of CIT against the weaknesses of the clash of civilizations thesis, the study constructed CIT as a single overarching framework and traced the overlap between the discernments obtained from the humanistic-existential model of psychology and the assertions of CIT.

In its attempt to forge a strong nexus between the twin paradigms of CIT, this study put forward the argument that the common emancipatory objectives of the 'production' and 'communication' paradigms of CIT emanated from a common broad intellectual project wherein the themes of *hegemony*, *reason* and *transcendence* played a central role. It asserted that the hegemonic elements of the production paradigm tended to owe their existence to the virtual speech community of the communication paradigm. The central significance of manufacturing acquiescence and legitimacy in the formation of a hegemonic order made it difficult to situate its existence entirely within the confines of the production paradigm. The reason backing the process of manufacturing acquiescence and legitimacy was largely shaped and contested within the boundaries of the communication paradigm. The principal battleground over which the struggle for hegemony was now occurring moved beyond the traditional Westphalian states-system. Cox's global civil society had a striking resemblance to Linklater's community of mankind as both reflected a cosmopolitan outlook.

After highlighting the connectivity between the dual paradigms of CIT, the study went further to map out the common characteristics of the humanistic-existential model of psychology and CIT. The humanistic-existential model of psychology held that the interplay of agency and structure characterised the collective understanding of ontology at different historical junctures. Such an approach to ontology found expression in the writings of CIT. Cox opined that ontologies were the parameters of our existence. He argued that reality was constructed by human minds which in turn were shaped by the complex of social relations. Linklater admitted that the capacities of human minds were linked inextricably with the forms of life in which they were involved. The modifications of human minds went hand-in-hand with the course of human history and therefore ontologies were not arbitrary constructions but the specifications of the common sense of an epoch.

The study derived four lessons from this common line of thinking that underpinned CIT and the humanistic-existential model of psychology. First, the ontology was constructed *collectively*, not individually. Second, the ontology existed in *plurality*, not singularity. Third, the process of establishing a dominant ontology was marked by *contestation*, not unanimity. Fourth, the dominant ontology was *dynamic*, not static. This understanding of ontology as a collective, pluralised, contested, and dynamic enterprise enabled CIT not only to expose the inadequacies of Huntington's thesis but also to emerge as a more consistent and comprehensive alternative theoretical framework.

In contrast to the post-positivist tilt of CIT, the positivist methodology of Huntington mistakenly treated ontology not as a dynamic construct but as a static entity which was essentially deterministic, ahistoric and immobile. Therefore, for Huntington, the dominant ontology that supported the notion of a prospective clash of civilizations was not an outcome of the *time and space sensitive* contestation between diverse collective human responses to varied conditions of existence, but a temporally and spatially neutral observation that had to be passively accepted. The historically and geographically determined causal mechanisms underlying the dominant ontology of civilizational clash remained undiagnosed by Huntington. This technical mistake accounted for a serious ethical failure. In the process of taking the dominant ontology of civilizational clash as granted, Huntington ended up *reinforcing* a conflictive world order rather than explaining it. What presented itself initially as the *explanandum* – the world order fraught with a civilizational clash as the developing outcome of some historical process (i.e. the end of the ideological clash associated with the Cold War) – was progressively transformed into the *explanan* as it was the civilizational clash which now explained the changing character of the world order and informed the foreign policy orientation of the states that wished to survive within it. Huntington's thesis was trapped in what Rosenberg called 'empty circularity'. The chance of surpassing this hellish state of affairs was totally circumscribed by Huntington. While the critics who did not subscribe to CIT considered Huntington's mistake as *accidental* and therefore began with finding fault in the epistemology (realist, orientalist, and elitist) and/or methodology (monolithic, inconsistent, and reductionist/ essentialist) of the clash of civilizations thesis, CIT attempted to uncover the hidden purposeful designs of Huntington and his supporters and suggested that Huntington's mistake was *intentional* as theories were always meant for serving particular purposes.

CIT's post-positivist orientation enabled it to overcome the methodological deficiencies of Huntington's thesis and carve out an alternative that was *technically efficient* and *ethically sound.* The technical efficiency and ethical soundness of CIT germinated from its flexible theoretical tool that ensured two advantages. First, it combined the moments of 'synchronic' and 'diachronic' analysis to provide a time and space sensitive explanation of the social reality. While the synchronic analysis had status-quoist tendencies as it is intended to correct the problems of the existing social order while retaining its base, the addition of the diachronic analysis to it allowed for a normative choice in favour of a social and political order different from the prevailing order. As such, CIT promised to prove useful not only in grasping the evolution of an ever changing social order but also in *influencing* and *channelling* the process of social change. CIT's move towards a new social order was not motivated by the idea of serving narrow self-interests but by a broad humane interest in enlightenment and emancipation. By relentlessly focusing on the question of emancipation and by questioning what this might mean in terms of the theory and practice of world politics, CIT successfully crossed Huntingtonian limits to a desirable social transformation that might be instrumental in building a peaceful world order.

Second, unlike Huntington's thesis, CIT did not convert the explanandum into explanan and therefore was free from the vice of empty circularity. In order to avoid empty circularity, Rosenberg had recommended that the explanation must fall back on some more basic social theory which could clarify as to why the phenomenon which was being explained became such a distinctive and salient feature of the contemporary world. The study showed that CIT could serve as the more basic social theory which could explain why the phenomenon of 'civilizational clash' gained momentum in the present era. The production paradigm of CIT could throw light on the disguised political and economic factors working behind what appeared as the 'civilizational conflict' while the communication paradigm of CIT could reveal the concealed impact of the ruptures or distortions in dialogue on the aggravation of the so-called civilizational tensions. On the basis of the insights drawn from its overarching theoretical tool, CIT could take a step further in the direction of formulating a *practical agenda* for socio-political transformation and emancipation. Guided by these theoretical and strategic merits, the study set out to apply CIT to provide an alternative and more accurate understanding of post-9/11 Afghanistan.

Post-9/11 Afghanistan: A Venue for Clashing Hegemonic Aspirations

The study employed CIT not only to provide an alternative and finer vision of the post-9/11 Afghan crisis, but also to suggest a way out of it. Cox's production paradigm was activated to demonstrate the hegemonic shifts in Afghan politics. Linklater's communication paradigm was operationalised to trace the linkage of these hegemonic shifts with the dialogic tensions in Afghan society. The alternative understanding derived from the application of these two paradigms reconstructed the post-9/11 Afghan scenario as an instance of a clash of hegemonic aspirations. Finally, the study recommended critical solutions for resolving so-called civilizational problems in post-9/11 Afghanistan.

For activating the Coxian theoretical scheme in order to mark the hegemonic shifts in post-9/11 Afghan politics, the study raised two questions: First, how did specific historical moments in national and global politics (structure) and collective human responses to them (agency) promote temporary coalitions of diverse hegemonic social forces in Afghanistan?; Second, how did the innate contradictions in these hegemonic coalitions develop, thereby historically transforming Afghan politics from one hegemonic phase to another? Since the post-9/11 Afghan scenario was largely a culmination of political events that began with the Soviet occupation of Afghanistan in the late 1970s, the study situated the above-mentioned questions against that historical backdrop. It was observed that the Soviet intervention in Afghanistan had a disturbing effect on both national (Afghan) politics and global politics. Its atheistic orientation threatened the hegemony of Islamists at the national level and its communist commitment generated insecurity for US hegemony at the global level. In its attempt to counter the Soviet influence in Afghanistan, the US began to support the Islamists, or the Mujahideen who had already been organising themselves against the Soviet-backed Leftist regime. This was a historical moment underlined by the temporary coalition of two diverse hegemonic social forces in Afghanistan: First, the Mujahideen dominated by ethnic Pashtuns who had hegemonised Afghanistan since its origin as a modern nation-state in 1747; Second, the Americans who had hegemonised the globe since the end of the Second World War in 1945.

Contradictions in this hegemonic coalition cropped up with the withdrawal of the Soviet forces and the end of the Cold War. The collapse of the Soviet Union reduced US interest in Afghanistan and deprived the Mujahideen of their common enemy. In the absence of a common enemy, the Pashtun-dominated political organisations of Mujahideen separated, thereby causing a split in the national hegemony of Pashtuns. The split in national hegemony caused a civil war which was characterised by several disjointed counter-hegemonic struggles wherein different non-Pashtun ethnic groups began to make their separate efforts to challenge the traditional Pashtun hegemony in Afghan politics. The study pointed out that the non-Pashtuns could not effectively challenge Pashtun hegemony as they failed to provide an agenda for generating an alternative knowledge-base and the corresponding social relations of production. By contrast, the Pashtuns, who had reorganised under the aegis of the Taliban and al-Qaida, evoked 'Sharia' as the alternative source of knowledge. They introduced alternative social relations of production whereby the localised predatory warlordism of the pre-Taliban era was replaced with a weak kind of rentier state power based on a criminalised open economy. The khan-dominated subsistence and local-trade economy was removed to establish a warlord-dominated commercial agriculture. This provided the newly armed elite (the Taliban) with the opportunity to mobilise resources to exercise power directly as it never had before. The Afghans, who were desperately looking for peace after facing a long civil war, chose to accept the alternative offered by the Taliban and al-Qaida, even if it meant re-asserting Pashtun hegemony in Afghan politics.

The US, that initially had no objection to the rise of Pashtun hegemony under the leadership of the Taliban and al-Qaida, gradually became critical of it as its aggressive acts had started affecting areas beyond the frontiers of Afghanistan. The terrorist attacks of 9/11 provoked the long-standing anguish of the US and the declaration of war on terror in Afghanistan was its violent outcome. This was a peculiar historical juncture that witnessed a direct confrontation between the same national and global hegemonic forces that had once formed a temporary coalition in Afghanistan. Now their hegemonic aspirations clashed with each other. In this clash of hegemonic aspirations, the US and the Taliban/al-Qaida generated their own versions of the dominant form of knowledge. While sources in the US propagated the clash of civilizations doctrine, the Taliban/al-Qaida disseminated a similar Jihadist ideology. The study pointed out that though these hegemonic discourses continued to grasp the psyche of a large section of people across the globe, their gradually weakening influence became apparent in the increasing use of force by both the US and the Taliban/al-Qaida. While they occasionally exercised force against each other, they also counted on each other for carrying out various fraudulent activities, opium cultivation being one of them. The study observed that the deep-rooted corruption in post-9/11 Afghan politics had not only created confusion but had also generated apathy in Afghan civil society. Though the presence of some progressive elements in Afghan civil society could not be denied, the study asserted that their uncoordinated and at times hidden efforts were hardly organised around a supporting alternative knowledge-base and alternative social relations of production. These efforts were therefore hardly sufficient to take the shape of an effective counter-hegemonic struggle.

The study proceeded to explain these hegemonic shifts in Afghan politics in terms of the dialogic tensions between Islamists and the West on the one hand, and between various Afghan ethnicities on the other. In this endeavour, the study posed two questions: first, on what normative grounds did the hegemonic discourses in post-9/11 Afghan history systematically include or exclude specific voices? Second, had the hitherto excluded voices been able to generate a 'moral capital' that could constitute the basis of a genuine counter-hegemonic struggle? These questions were examined in the context of two clearly identifiable phases of Pashtun hegemony in recent Afghan history. The first hegemonic phase appeared when the Pashtun-dominated Mujahideen joined hands to fight against the Soviets. The second hegemonic phase emerged when the Pashtuns reorganised under the Taliban and came together with al-Qaida to fight against the Americans.

During the first hegemonic phase, the hegemonic discourse produced by the Mujahideen promoted two norms: pro-Islam and anti-foreign. The Afghans, who were deeply religious and fiercely independent, quickly responded to the fatwa issued by the Mujahideen. However, a close reading of the fatwa found that the Mujahideen discourse was exclusionary on two grounds. First, it intended to exclude 'insincere Muslims' who were modernists or were under other non-Islamic political influence. Second, it totally closed the possibility of an open dialogue with non-Muslims as they were considered kafirs. The repercussions of this exclusionary attitude became visible at two levels. At the national level, the Muslim sentiment present in the Mujahideen discourse temporarily mobilised all the ethnic groups of Afghanistan against the Soviets, but its 'selective' Islamic preference resulted in the formation of a loose Islamic Alliance which soon collapsed after the withdrawal of Soviet troops from Afghanistan. At the global level, the principle of non-engagement with non-Muslims was not actually practiced by the Mujahideen. Despite the closed nature of the Mujahideen discourse, the Mujahideen movement sought external support not just from various Islamic states, but also from the US which was supposed to be treated as a kafir country as per Mujahideen standards. The gap between the verbal declarations and the practical strategy of the Mujahideen proved disastrous. The ethnic rivalry for receiving military and financial aid from diverse external sources caused feuding not only amongst the Pashtun-dominated organisations of the Mujahideen, but also amongst various Afghan ethnicities. This rivalry ultimately led to the fall of Pashtun hegemony and caused a civil war in Afghanistan.

While the civil war remained inconclusive, the Pashtuns began to reclaim their lost hegemonic status by launching the Taliban movement in a close alliance with al-Qaida. In this second phase of Pashtun hegemony, the hegemonic discourse generated by the Taliban/al-Qaida endorsed two norms: pro-martyrdom and anti-America. The Taliban/al-Qaida discourse indicated a rupture in the dialogic possibilities between the Islamists and the Americans, and tended to exclude the voices of those secular Muslims who lived in the West. The Taliban/al-Qaida also demonstrated exclusionary tendencies towards the Shia Hazaras. The excesses committed during the Taliban regime attracted criticisms from all corners of the world. Despite the growing worldwide criticism, the Taliban/al-Qaida continued to spread destruction and to push their hegemonic discourse. They proudly took responsibility for the terrorist attacks of 9/11, but when their pride in killing Americans was not shared by many religious leaders in Islamic societies, they denied any involvement in it. At one moment, they described themselves as anti-America and not as anti-Americans, and at another moment they claimed to be both. The contradictory statements released by them disseminated distorted meanings in the Afghan dialogic community. The dialogic distortions created by the Taliban/al-Qaida seriously undermined their consensual legitimacy. The sudden undermining of consensual legitimacy resulted in greatly weakening their hegemony. Consequently, post-9/11 Afghan politics totally discarded the voice of the Taliban and took notice of only those anti-Taliban voices that had organised themselves under the aegis of the US-backed Northern Alliance.

However, the study highlighted that in the years following 9/11 the leaders of the Northern Alliance in Afghanistan gradually shifted their attitudes towards the Taliban. There had been a renewal in the ties between the Northern Alliance and the Taliban on the one hand, and a growing distance in relations between the Taliban and al-Qaida, on the other. The confusing shifts in allegiances blurred the Afghan dialogic space. A good number of Afghans had lost their faith in the utility of dialogue. Though the critical voices of Afghan NGOs, INGOs, inter-governmental organisations, academic institutions, and donor governments had made a remarkable entry into the Afghan dialogic community, they failed to generate a unified discourse. In the absence of a unified discourse, the anti-hegemonic moral capital remained under-exploited. The study declared that post-9/11 Afghanistan stood at a crossroads marked by complex interactions between feebly hegemonic, as well as aspiring, counter-hegemonic social forces.

In its attempt to find an exit from this troubling state of affairs, the study recommended the organisation of an effective counter-hegemonic struggle against both the national Pashtun hegemony and the global US hegemony. This demanded the designing of an *alternative knowledge-base,* the organisation of the critical social forces along *alternative social relations of production,* and the creation of an *all-inclusive speech community*. The study considered the philosophical tenets of the Quran as the potential source of an alternative knowledge-base in post-9/11 Afghan politics. It held that the adherence to Islamic philosophy would provide a check on the conceits of religious power and would advocate 'inter-faith' discussions on Islam, thereby laying the foundation for an all-inclusive Afghan dialogic community. The philosophical approach to the Quran would create ample space for a passionate dialogue between followers of religious, spiritual, and secular Islamic traditions. An open dialogue between various Islamic and non-Islamic voices would differently inform the common consciousness of Afghans. The common consciousness raised by the cross-fertilisation of varied Islamic interpretations would transcend that concept of Islamism which sees it as an exclusivist and totalising ideology, thereby promoting a 'post-Islamic' current that would espouse inclusion and pluralism. The post-Islamic ideology would demand equal basic civil rights for all Muslim and non-Muslim residents of Afghanistan and would attempt to organise them along alternative social relations of production.

The study suggested that a preliminary post-Islamic agenda for establishing alternative social relations of production could draw inspiration from Michael Lowy's idea of 'elective affinity' that demonstrated how Christianity had turned into the institutionalised ideology of communistic utopianism in Latin America. Based on the Latin American model of Christian liberation theology, the study asserted that the critical social forces in post-9/11 Afghanistan must strive to construct a post-Islamic liberation theology that could permit Islam to breed such governmental institutions that could redress the grievances of the poor Afghans and genuinely work for transforming their miserable conditions of existence. The study concluded that the humanistic re-interpretation of the Quran by the post-Islamic counter-hegemonic forces in Afghanistan would not only pave the way for transforming the post-9/11 Afghan crisis, but would also be a crucial step towards vindicating Islam against its distortion and demonisation by both Muslim and non-Muslim hegemonic aspirants in the contemporary world.

APPENDIX I

Pen-Portraits and Organisation Profiles

Selay Ghaffar, Humanitarian Assistance for the Women and Children of Afghanistan (HAWCA).

Selay Ghaffar is the Executive Director of HAWCA (http://www.hawca.org). She is an industrious women's rights activist and sits on the executive board of the Afghan Women's Network (AWN), a key umbrella group for women's rights organisations in Afghanistan. Her commitment to efforts to eliminate violence against women includes cooperation with the Ministry of Women Affairs in drafting Afghanistan's first Elimination of Violence Against Women (EVAW) law, recently signed by the President Hamid Karzai. She is a frequent participant at global women's rights meetings. She has a special expertise on UN-Resolution 1325, human rights law and women's role in conflict-resolution. She served as a member of the official delegation to Geneva for the presentation of the Universal Period Report on Human Rights (UPR) of the Islamic Republic of Afghanistan. She has been a member of the group of youths who were active since 1992 doing volunteer work in Afghan refugee camps in Pakistan. After seven years of sporadic work they decided to organise themselves which resulted in the foundation of HAWCA in 1999. HAWCA's establishment was motivated by the despair and devastation suffered by Afghan women and children as victims of war and injustice in Afghanistan and as refugees in Pakistan. HAWCA has devoted its efforts to improving the lives of Afghans under difficult circumstances, from the era of Taliban domination to today's insecure Afghanistan, and is a deserving recipient of many prestigious awards – Isabel Ferror's Award, Amnesty International Award and Primo Donne Award – for the commendable job it has done over the years.

Andeisha Farid, Afghan Child Education and Care Organisation (AFCECO).

Andeisha Farid is the Founder and Executive Director of AFCECO (http://www.afceco.org). After the Soviet invasion, she was forced to temporarily settle at a camp in Iran. She moved to Pakistan to study initially at the refugee camp and later at the Islamabad University. During her stay in Pakistan, she began to tutor Afghan widows and children who had no place to learn. Touched by the misery of Afghan street children in Islamabad, she collected fund from the local community to establish a safe place where street children could live and study. With assistance from Charity Help International (CHI), a US-based NGO, Andeisha was able to open her first orphanage in Pakistan. Today, AFCECO runs 11 orphanages in Afghanistan and refugee camps in Pakistan with 600 children of diverse ethnicities and has employed nearly 200 people who are mostly widows and university students. Andeisha was honoured with the Global Leadership Award of Vital Voices, the Goldman Sachs and the *Fortune* Global Women Leaders Mentoring Award at Fortune Most Powerful Women Summit 2010. Andeisha's AFCECO instils important leadership values of tolerance and an appreciation for education in Afghanistan's future generation.

Shahla Farid, University of Kabul and Afghan Women's Network (AWN).

Shahla Farid is a Professor at the Faculty of Law in Kabul University. She is a writer and a women right activist. She has also been on the executive board of *Afghan Women's Network* (http://www.afghanwomensnetwork.org). The AWN is a non-profit network of women and women's NGOs working to empower the women of Afghanistan and ensure their equal participation in Afghan society. In 2003, Shahla wrote a book about Gender and Laws in Afghanistan. After its publication she was threatened and went into hiding for three years. In 2006, she wrote another book funded by '*Action Aid Afghanistan*' examining women's rights in Islam. She has worked for Ariana Television and presented a programme discussing various women's issues.

Maduda (name changed), Revolutionary Association of the Women of Afghanistan (RAWA).

RAWA (http://www.rawa.org) is a women's organisation based in Quetta, Pakistan, that promotes women's rights and secular democracy. It was founded in 1977 by Meena Keshwar Kamal, an Afghan student activist who was assassinated in 1987 for her political activities. The group, which supports non-violent strategies, had its initial office in Kabul, Afghanistan, but then moved to Pakistan in the early 1980s. The group opposed the Soviet-supported government and the following Mujahideen and Taliban Islamist governments in Afghanistan. It continues to oppose the present US-supported Islamic Republican form of the Northern Alliance government. RAWA holds that the US-led war on terrorism removed the Taliban regime in October 2001, but it has not removed religious fundamentalism. In fact, by reinstalling the warlords in power in Afghanistan, the US administration is replacing one fundamentalist regime with another. The US government and President Karzai mostly rely on Northern Alliance criminal leaders who are as brutal and misogynist as the Taliban. RAWA realises the need for tremendous social and relief work amongst unimaginably traumatised Afghan women and children, but unfortunately it does not at the moment enjoy any support from international NGOs or governments. Due to lack of funds, it cannot run its humanitarian projects as effectively as it wishes. RAWA believes that freedom and democracy can't be donated; it is the duty of the people of a country to fight and achieve these values. RAWA has so far won 16 awards and certificates from around the world for its work for human rights and democracy including the sixth Asian Human Rights Award, the French Republic's Liberty, Equality, Fraternity Human Rights Prize, Islamabad Emma Humphries Memorial Prize, SAIS-Novartis International Journalism Award from Johns Hopkins University, Certificate of Special Congressional Recognition from the U.S. Congress and Honorary Doctorate from University of Antwerp (Belgium) for outstanding non-academic achievements.

Saifuddin Saihoon, University of Kabul.

Saifuddin Saihoon is a Professor of Political Economy at Kabul University. Being one of the most distinguished economists of contemporary Afghanistan, he is often called by President Karzai to render his expert advice on economic matters. His views on Afghan economic issues capture wide coverage in national as well as international media. He links economy with social life and holds the opinion that social welfare including access to health and education cannot be achieved until Afghanistan solves the security problems that are generated by a massive black market, run with the collusion of politicians and protected by armed militia. He advocates the idea of a dynamic and sustainable economic development.

Daud Razmak, Afghanistan Solidarity Party (ASP).

Daud Razmak is the Chairman of ASP which aims at attaining independence and establishing a warlord-free democratic government in Afghanistan. It works for uniting the Afghans, liberating them from foreign control and alleviating their poverty by pushing the demand for transferring money from corrupt warlords to poor Afghans. The ASP stands for establishment of a democratic and secular society, protection of women's rights, freedom of the press and disarmament of the country. Formed in 2004, the ASP has its roots in Maoist parties which were composed of anti-Soviet Marxists and socialists in Afghanistan. The ASP, which is active in most of Afghanistan's 34 provinces, operates as a coalition of six parties and forms a part of a larger association of like-minded secular parties oriented towards democracy. ASP has won support of well-known Afghan activists like Malalai Joya. The Canada-Afghan Solidarity Committee has helped raise money for ASP.

Baryalai Fetrat, University of Kabul.

Baryalai Fetrat is a Professor at the Department of Sociology in Kabul University. Kabul University is the oldest and largest institution of tertiary education in Afghanistan. Since 1932, it has not only provided training to a large number of Afghans but has enjoyed popularity in the region by attracting many students from neighbouring countries. The Faculty of Social Science was separated from the Faculty of Literature and was independently founded in 1980. The Department of Sociology is currently located within the Faculty of Social Science in Kabul University.

Najla Ayubi, Asia Foundation, Afghanistan Office.

Najla Ayubi has been a Judge and is the Program Director for Law, Human Rights, and Women's Empowerment in the Asia Foundation's Afghanistan office. She contributed greatly to crucial programming efforts including co-authoring the 2011 and 2010 Survey of the Afghan People. Ayubi is a former prosecutor and Commissioner of the Independent Election Commission (IEC) and the Joint Electoral Management Body (JEMB) of Afghanistan, and also served as a Legal Advisor to the State Ministry for Parliamentary Affairs within the Afghan Government. Ayubi was recently made the Country Director for the Open Society Foundation's (OSF's) Afghanistan office. Prior to joining the Asia Foundation, from 2006-2007, she was an OSI Chevening scholar at the University of York, where she completed her Master's degree in Post-War Recovery and Development Studies. Ayubi is the executive board member of Afghan Woman's Network and the global advisory board member of South Asia Women's Regional Network.

Abdul Latif Rasif, Kabul Court.

Abdul Latif Rasif is a Law Advisor and Judge at the Kabul Court. In accordance with article 116 of the Afghan Constitution, the judiciary is an independent body of the Islamic Republic of Afghanistan. The judicial power is comprised of the Supreme Court, Appeal Courts and Primary Courts, the authorities of which are regulated by law. Rasif is highly critical of the position of judiciary in contemporary Afghanistan. He opines that though the judiciary has an independent character in principle, it remains dependent in practice and the rule of law does not exist in Afghanistan.

Bulqis Roshan, Provincial Council of Farah Province, Afghanistan.

Bulqis Roshan is a Senator of the Provincial Council of Farah province of Afghanistan. She is a sociology graduate as well as a law student. She worked as a teacher and headed a hospital in Farah province. Roshan currently lives in Kabul and is a staunch critic of the corrupt Karzai regime. She has not acquired the membership of any political party. She is an independent candidate who accepts the opinion of parties that stand for the people of Afghanistan.

Fauzia Amini, Legal Department of Ministry of Women Affairs, Government of Afghanistan.

Fauzia Amini is the Head of the Legal Department of Ministry of Women Affairs. The Afghan Ministry of Women's Affairs (MOWA) is a new ministry in the Afghan government which was set up in 2001. The Minister heading the MOWA reports directly to the President and is a member of the Cabinet. MOWA leadership envisions the Ministry as a policy-making body and relies with little success on other ministries for implementing its programmes. As per Wikileaks, civil society actors largely agree that MOWA is a weak advocate for Afghan women (http://www.cablegatesearch.net/cable.php?id=08KABUL3342). Amini's reluctance to freely share her views during the interview and her decision to abruptly end it clearly indicated the limitations of MOWA.

Wahid Paikan, BBC, Kabul.

Wahid Paikan is a journalist who works for BBC-Persian in Kabul. He advocates freedom of journalism in Afghanistan. He opines that journalists are responsible for informing people about political issues. Since journalists are impartial, they must be allowed by all those who have political and military power to perform their duty without any restrictions. He is extremely critical of the alarming rates of intimidation, harassment and detention of practicing journalists in Afghanistan.

Ravi Ramakrishna, Indian Information Service, Government of India.

Ravi Ramakrishna is an Indian bureaucrat currently posted at Kabul. Before joining as capacity development advisor to the Ministry of Information, Government of Afghanistan, he had worked in Kabul as correspondent of Doordarshan.

Siddharth Dev Verman, Indian Administrative Service, Government of India.

Siddharth Dev Verman is an Indian bureaucrat presently posted at Kabul. Before joining as capacity development advisor to the Ministry of Labour, Government of Afghanistan, he worked as Joint Secretary in the Ministry of Labour, Government of India.

Ian Pounds, American Educator and Volunteer at AFCECO.

Ian Pounds is an American Educator who has now permanently shifted to Afghanistan for serving its war-torn society. In Afghanistan, one out of every twelve children have lost both of their parents. Seven out of ten people are illiterate. Knowing this, Ian has committed himself to supporting these children, even at the risk of his own life. In 2009, he spent five months living and working as a volunteer at Mehan Orphanage in Kabul. It was an experience that affected him deeply. He presently works as the Education Director at AFCECO. He teaches English, drama, photography and computer skills to hundreds of the Afghan orphans. Ian recently visited across the US to raise awareness and support for AFCECO's vision for a free and secure Afghanistan.

Gloria Geretto, Italian Volunteer at AFCECO.

Gloria Geretto is a graduate in linguistics from University of Florence, Italy. She worked as a volunteer at AFCECO for a couple of months. She taught English to Afghan children in the orphanages. She is currently pursuing her Masters in Refugee Care from University of Essex.

Najib, Activist at HAWCA.

Najib is a graduate from Kabul University and currently works on various humanitarian projects of HAWCA.

APPENDIX II

Sample Questionnaire

1. Afghan society has a long history of conflict. The nature of this conflict has transformed over time. Is there an identifiable root cause behind this conflict or are there different causes that have been responsible for generating conflict at different points in time?

2. What role is played by religion/culture/civilization in shaping the conflict in Afghanistan? Does the majority in Afghanistan view the ongoing conflict as a clash of civilizations? Does the opinion of elites differ from that of the masses in this regard?

3. How do different sections of Afghan society react to the idea of 'war on terror' and to the presence of foreign forces in post-9/11 Afghanistan?

4. What are the economic repercussions of the war on terror in Afghanistan? How has it affected the traditional relations of production in Afghan society?

5. Who are the beneficiaries of the Afghan war economy? Do they belong to certain or specific ethnic/religious/political group?

6. Are the economically dominant groups of Afghan society also politically dominant?

7. Are the interests of the dominant groups of Afghan society and those of the foreign forces present in post-9/11 Afghanistan basically the same? Do these foreign forces have a unified political agenda?

8. Is the Afghan media free from foreign control? How influential is it in determining the dynamics of Afghan civil society?

9. How does Afghan civil society influence the activities of the Afghan state? Do the bureaucrats take into account the public opinion before making

policy decisions?

10. Despite the fragmentation of Afghan civil society along ethnic/regional/religious/linguistic lines, does the Afghan state remain unified? What is the cementing factor or factors that bind Afghan society together?

11. How can the ongoing conflict in Afghanistan be resolved? Can 'dialogue' between the warring camps be an effective medium for establishing peace?

12. What is your view about the role played by the neighbouring countries in the ongoing conflict? Can any or some or all of these neighbours be part of the solution to the conflict?

Bibliography

Acharya, Amitav 2002 'Clash of Civilizations? No, of National Interests and Principles'. Available at http://www.cpdsindia.org/clashofcivilizations.htm

Achcar, Gilbert 2004 *Eastern Cauldron,* Monthly Review Press.

Achcar, Gilbert 2008 'Religion and Politics Today From a Marxian Perspective', *Socialist Register*, pp. 55-76.

Adorno, Theodore W. 2001 *Problems of Moral Philosophy* edited by Thomas Schroder, translated by Rodney Livingstone, Stanford University Press.

Ahmad, Aijaz 2008 'Islam, Islamisms and the West', *Socialist Register.* Vol. 44. Available at http://socialistregister.com/index.php/srv/article/view/5873#. WHH0Nht97IU

Ahrari, M.E. 1997 'The Clash of Civilizations: An Old Story or New Truth?', *New Perspectives Quarterly*, Vol. 14. No. 2, pp. 56-61.

Aitchison, C. U. (ed.) 1909, Vol. II, *A Collection of Treaties, Engagement and Sanads Relating to India and Neighbouring Countries,* Calcutta.

Ajami, Fouad September- October 1993 'The Summoning', *Foreign Affairs,* Vol. 72, No. 4, pp. 2-9.

Akhtar, Shabbir 2008 *The Quran and the Secular Mind: A Philosophy of Islam,* Routledge.

Alam, M. Shahid 2003 'Is this a Clash of Civilizations?'. Available at http://www.mediamonitors.net/mshahidalam2.html

Alexander, Yonah and Michael S. Swetnam 2001 *Usama bin Laden's al-Qaida: Profile of a Terrorist Network,* Transnational Publishers.

Ali Mukhtar Ahmad 2002 'Towards Peace and Reconciliation in Afghanistan: A Pakistani Perspective', *Peace Initiatives*, Vol. 3, Nos. 1-3, pp. 79-90.

Ambassador Michael Sheehan, 12 July, 2000 Office of the Coordinator for Counter Terrorism, *Testimony Before the House International Relations Committee*, Washington, DC.

Anderson, Perry 1976 'The Antinomies of Antonio Gramsci', *New Left Review,* Vol.1, No. 100, pp. 1-78.

Anderson, Perry 2005 *Spectrum,* Verso.

Anievas, Alexander 2008 Review Articles, *Historical Materialism,* Vol. 16, pp. 167-236.

Anwar, Raja 1998 *The Tragedy of Afghanistan*, Verso.

Arasli, Jahangir 2011 'States vs. Non-State Actors: Asymmetric Conflict of the 21st Century and Challenges to Military Transformation', INEGMA Special Report No. 13. Available at http://www.inegma.com/Admin/Content/File-81020131379.pdf

Arjomand, Said Amir 2007 'Can Rational Analysis Break a Taboo?: A Middle Eastern Perspective'. Available at http://essays.ssrc.org/sept11/essays/arjomand.htm

Arkoun, M. 1988 'The Concept of Authority in Islamic Thought' in Ferdinand K. and Mozaffari, M. (eds.) *Islam, State and Society*, Curzon Press.

Aron, Raymond 1966 *Peace and War: A Theory of International Relations,* Weidenfeld and Nicholson.

Asadi, Mohammad 2007 'A Critique of Huntington's Clash of Civilizations'. Available at http://archive.li/Eq7sVl

Azzam, Shaikh Abdullah 2002 'Defence of the Muslim Lands: The First Obligation after Iman' available at http://www.religioscope.com/info/doc/jihad/azzam_defence_1_table.htm

Azzam, Sheikh Abdullah 2003 *The Lofty Mountain, Azzam Publications.*

Barber, Benjamin 2003 *Jihad vs. Mcworld*, Corgi.

Bayat, Asef 2008 'Islamism and Empire: The Incongruous Nature of Islamist Anti-Imperialism', *Socialist Register,* pp. 38-54.

Bayat, Asef 2011 'The Post-Islamist Revolutions', *Foreign Affairs.* Available at http://www.foreignaffairs.com/articles/67812/asef-bayat/the-post-islamist-revolutions

Bennis, Phyllis 2009 'President Obama's Afghanistan Escalation Speech: An Assessment'. Available at https://www.tni.org/es/node/13231

Benoit Jean-Louis 2007 *Notes sur le Coran et Autres Textes sur les Religions (Notes on the Koran and Other Texts on Religion) by Alexis de Tocqueville*, Bayard.

Bernstein, R. 1976 *The Restructuring of Social and Political Theory,* Oxford.

Besteman, Catherine Lowe and Hugh Gusterson 2005 *Why America's Top Pundits are Wrong*, University of California Press.

Blanton, Stephen 2011 *The Heart of Islam,* Author House.

Bloom, William 1990 *Personal Identity, National Identity and International Relations,* Cambridge.

Bonner, Michael David 2005 'Poverty and Economics in the Qur'an', *Journal of Interdisciplinary History*, Vol.35, No.3, pp. 391-406.

Bronner, Stephen Eric 2011 'On Judging American Foreign Policy: Human Rights, Political Realism and the Arrogance of Power', *Logos: A Journal of Modern Society and Culture*. Available at http://logosjournal.com/2011/summer_bronner/

Brown, Christopher Leslie 2006 *Moral Capital: Foundations of British Abolitionism*, UNC Press Books.

Bruderlein, Claude, Khalil Shariff, Jolyon Leslie, Adeel Ahmad and Timea Szabo 2002 'The Role of Islam in Shaping the Future of Afghanistan', *Peace Initiatives,* Vol. 8, Nos. 1-3, pp.44-55.

Budd, Adrian 2007 'Gramsci's Marxism and International Relations', *International Socialism*, Issue 114. Available at http://www.isj.org.uk/index.php4?id=309&issue=114

Buhler, C. and M. Allen 1972 *Introduction to Humanistic Psychology*, Brooks / Cole.

Callinicos, Alex 2007 'Does Capitalism Need the State System?', *Cambridge Review of International Affairs,* Vol. 20, No. 4, pp. 533-549.

Centlivres, Pierre and Centlivres-Demont Micheline 1998 'Tajikistan and Afghanistan: The Ethnic Groups on Either Side of the Border' in Djalili, Mohammad-Reza, Grare, F. and Akiner, Shirin (eds.) *Tajikistan: the Trials of Independence,* Richmond: Curzon.

Chapman, Steve September 8, 2011 'Who Kept Us Safe After 9/11?', *Chicago Tribune.* Available at http://articles.chicagotribune.com/2011-09-08/news/ct-oped-0908-chapman-20110908_1_terrorist-attacks-car-bomb-domestic-terrorism

Chatterjee, Pratap 2010 'Paying Off the Warlords: Anatomy of a Culture of Corruption' and Roston, Aram 2010 'How the US Funds the Taliban' in Turse, Nick (ed.) *The Case for Withdrawal from Afghanistan*, Verso, pp. 81-95.

Chossudovsky, Michel February 26, 2016 'Al Qaeda and the War on Terrorism', Global Research available at http://www.globalresearch.ca/al-qaeda-and-the-war-on-terrorism/7718

Clements, Frank A. 2003 *Conflict in Afghanistan: An Encyclopaedia*, ABC-CLIO.

Commins, David 1996 'Osama bin Laden's Declaration of Jihad Against Americans', *Milestone Documents in World History: Exploring the Primary Sources that Shaped the World.* Available at http://salempress.com/store/pdfs/bin_Laden.pdf

Cox, Robert W. 1981 'Social Forces, States and World Order: Beyond International Relations Theory', *Millennium,* Vol.10, No.2, pp. 126-155.

Cox, Robert W. 1987 *Production, Power and World Order: Social Forces in the Making of History,* Columbia University Press.

Cox, Robert W. 1992 'Towards a Post-hegemonic Conceptualization of World Order' in James N. Rosenau and Ernest Otto-Czempiel (eds.) *Governance Without Government: Order and Change in World Politics,* Cambridge.

Cox, Robert W. 1992 *'Globalization, Multilateralism and Democracy'*, the John Holmes Memorial Lecture delivered to the conference of the Academic Council of the United States System, Washington D.C.

Cox, Robert W. 1993 *'Critical Political Economy'*, lecture given to the United Nations University conference on Emerging Trends in Political Economy and International Relations Theory, Oslo, Norway.

Cox, Robert W. and Timothy Sinclair (eds.) 1996 *Approaches to World Order,* Cambridge.

Cox, Robert W. and Michael G. Schechter 2002 *The Political Economy of a Plural World: Critical Reflections on Power, Morals and Civilization,* Routledge.

Cox, Robert W. 2005 'Global Perestroika' in Rorden Wilkinson (ed.), *The Global Governance Reader*, Routledge.

Cordovez, D. and Harrison S. S. 1995 *Out of Afghanistan: The Inside Story of the Soviet Withdrawal,* Oxford University Press.

Dale, Roger and Susan Robertson 2003 'Interview with Robert W. Cox', *Globalisation, Societies and Education.* Available at http://seriesofhopes.files. wordpress.com/2008/05/interview-cox.pdf

Das, Sukanya Mohan 2002 'Process Issues: An Argument for Inclusion of Grass-roots Communities in the Formulation of National and International Initiatives in Re-building Afghanistan', *Peace Initiatives*, Vol. 3, Nos. 1-3, pp. 30-43.

Dorraj, Manochehr December 1998 'In the Throes of Civilizational Conflict', *Peace Review*, Vol. 10, No. 4, pp. 633-637.

Dunn, Michael 2006-2007 'The Clash of Civilizations and the War on Terror', *49th Parallel*, Vol. 20. Available at http://www.49thparallel.bham.ac.uk/back/ issue20/Dunn.pdf

Dupree, Louis 1980 'Red Flag over the Hindu Kush pt.3: Rhetoric and Reforms, or Promises! Promises!' American Universities Field Staff Report 23.

Duvall, Raymond and Varadarajan, Latha 2003 'On the Practical Significance of Critical International Relations Theory', *Asian Journal of Political Science,* Vol. 11, Issue 2, pp. 75-88.

Elster, Jon 1983 *Sour Grapes,* Cambridge.

Elphinstone, Mountstuart 1972 *An Account of the Kingdom of Caubul*, Vol.1, Oxford University Press.

Englehardt, Tom 2010 'Going for Broke: Six Ways the Af-Pak War is Expanding' in Turse, Nick (ed.) *The Case for Withdrawal from Afghanistan*, Verso, pp.115-125.

Ewans, Martin 2001 *Afghanistan: A New History,* Curzon Press.

Fabian, K. P. 2002 'The Politics of War', *Frontline,* Vol. 19, No. 2. Available at http://www.hindu.com/fline/fl1902/fl190200.htm

Filkins, Dexter Jan 24, 2010 'U.N. Seeks to Drop Some Taliban From Terror List', *The New York Times*. Available at http://www.nytimes.com/2010/01/25/world/asia/25taliban.html

Flounders, Sara December 2, 2009 'Obama's War: Why is the Largest Military Machine of the Planet Unable to Defeat the Resistance in Afghanistan?'. Available at http://www.globalresearch.ca/indexphp?context=va&aid=16354

Freud, Sigmund 1953 *Civilization and its Discontents*, Hogarth Press (originally published in 1930).

Freud, Sigmund 1961 *Future of an Illusion*, Hogarth Press (originally published in 1927).

Fromm, Eric P 1942 *Fear of Freedom,* Routledge.

Fromm, Eric 1955 *The Sane Society*, Fawcett Premier Books.

Fukuyama, Francis 1992 *The End of History and the Last Man*, Penguin.

Garthoff, Raymond L. 1994 *Detente and Confrontation: American-Soviet Relations from Nixon to Reagan,* Brookings Institution Press.

Germain, Randall D. and Kenny, Michael 1998 'Engaging Gramsci: International Relations Theory and the New Gramscians', *Review of International Studies,* Vol. 24, pp. 3-21.

Gill, Stephen 1993 'Epistemology, Ontology and the "Italian School"' in Gill, Stephen (ed.) *Gramsci, Historical Materialism and International Relations*, Cambridge University Press.

Glatzer, Bernt 1999 'Is Afghanistan on the Brink of Ethnic and Tribal Disintegration? in Maley, William (ed.) *Fundamentalism Reborn?: Afghanistan and the Taliban,* Hurst and Company.

Glatzer, Bernt 2002 'The Pashtun Tribal System' in Pfeffer, Georg and Behera, Deepak Kumar (eds.) *Concepts of Tribal Society,* Concept Publishing Co.

Griffin, Michael 2001 *Reaping the Whirlwind: The Taliban Movement in Afghanistan,* Pluto Press.

Griffith, John C. 1981 *Afghanistan: Key to A Continent*, Westview Press.

Goodarzi, Jubin November 13, 1996 'Washington and the Taliban', *Green Left Weekly.* Available at http://www.greenleft.org.au/node/13052

Goodhand, Jonathan 2004 'From War Economy to Peace Economy? Reconstruction and State Building in Afghanistan', *Journal of International Affairs,* Vol. 58, No. 1, pp. 155-174.

Goodin, Robert (ed.) 1996 *The Theory of Institutional Design,* Cambridge.

Goodson, Larry P. 2001 *Afghanistan's Endless War: State Failure, Regional Politics, and the Rise of the Taliban,* University of Washington Press.

Gopal, Anand December 7, 2009 'Taliban Seek Deal on Foreign Forays', *The Wall Street Journal.* Available at http://online.wsj.com/article/SB126002422466878409.html

Gramsci, Antonio 1971 *Selections from Prison Notebooks*, translated & edited by Quintin Hoare and Geoffrey Nowell Smith, International Publishers.

Griffin, David Ray May 29, 2013 'Osama bin Laden Responsible for the 9/11 Attacks? Where is the Evidence?', *Global Research*. Available at http://www.globalresearch.ca/osama-bin-laden-responsible-for-the-9-11-attacks-where-is-the-evidence/15892

Habermas, J. 1990 *Moral Consciousness and Communicative Action,* MIT Press.

Hall, Donald (ed.) 1982 *Claims for Poetry*, University of Michigan Press.

Halliday, Fred 1996 *Islam and the Myth of Confrontation,* I. B. Tauris.

Halliday, Fred 1996 *Islam and the Myth of Confrontation*, St. Martin's Press.

Hanson, Victor Davis 2001 *Carnage and Culture: Landmark Battles in the Rise of Western Power*, Anchor Books.

Hendrie, Edward 2011 *9/11 - Enemies Foreign and Domestic*, Great Mountain Publishing.

Heywood, Andrew 1994 *Political Ideas and Concepts: An Introduction,* Macmillan, p.101.

Hiro, Dilip 2002 *War Without End: The Rise of Islamic Terrorism and Global Response,* Routledge.

Hobson, John M. 2010 'To Be or Not to Be a Non-reductionist Marxist: Is that the Question?' in Anievas, Alexander (ed.) *Marxism and World Politics,* Routledge.

Hoff, Joan 2007 *A Faustian Foreign Policy from Woodrow Wilson to George W. Bush: Dreams of Perfectibility*, Cambridge University Press.

Honneth, Axel 1995 *The Struggle for Recognition: The Moral Grammar of Social Conflicts*, Polity Press.

Hooper, John and Kate Connolly September 27, 2001 'Berlusconi Breaks Ranks Over Islam', *The Guardian.* Available at http://www.guardian.co.uk/world/2001/sep/27/afghanistan.terrorism7

Howe, Richard Herbert 1978 'Max Weber's Elective Affinities: Sociology within the Bounds of Pure Reason', *American Journal of Sociology,* Vol. 84, No.2. Available at http://www.jstor.org/pss/2777853

Hunter, Shireen T. 1998 *The Future of Islam and the West: Clash of Civilizations or Peaceful Coexistence?,* Praeger.

Huntington, Samuel P. November- December 1993 'If Not Civilizations, What?: Paradigms of the Post- Cold War World', *Foreign Affairs,* pp.186-194.

Huntington, Samuel P. 1993 'The Clash of Civilizations?', *Foreign Affairs* Vol. 72, No. 3, pp. 21-49.

Huntington, Samuel P. November- December 1996 'The West Unique, Not Universal', *Foreign Affairs*, p. 45.

Huntington, Samuel P. 1996 *The Clash of Civilizations and the Remaking of World Order*, Penguin.

Hussein, Seifudein Adem 2001 'On the End of History and the Clash of Civilizations: A Dissenter's View', *Journal of Muslim Minority Affairs*, Vol. 21, No. 1, pp. 25-38. Available at http://lists.extropy.org/pipermail/paleopsych/2005-May/003271.html

Ikenberry , G. John March- April 1997 'The West: Precious, not Unique: Civilizations Make for a Poor Paradigm Just Like the Rest,' *Foreign Affairs*, Vol. 76, No. 2. Available at http://www.foreignaffairs.com/articles/52873/g-john-ikenberry-et-al/the-west-precious-not-unique-civilizations-make-for-a-poor-parad

Jalali, Ali Ahmad 2002 *Afghan Guerrilla Warfare: In the Words of the Mujahideen Fighters,* Zenith Press.

Jay, Martin 1984 *Adorno,* Fontana Press.

Jones, Richard Wyn 1999 *Security, Strategy and Critical Theory,* Lynne Reinner Publishers.

Jones, Richard Wyn (ed.) 2001 *Critical Theory and World Politics,* Lynne Reinner Publishers.

Jones, Schuyler 1974 *Men of Influence in Nuristan*, Seminar Press.

Kakar, M. Hasan 1973 *The Pacification of the Hazaras of Afghanistan,* Afghanistan Council, Asia Society.

Kalin, Ibrahim 2001 'Islam and the West: Deconstructing Monolithic Perceptions-A Conversation With Professor John Esposito' *Journal of Muslim Minority Affairs*, Vol. 21, No. 1, pp. 155-163.

Kane, John 2001 *The Politics of Moral Capital,* Cambridge University Press.

Katzenstein, Peter J. (ed.) 2010 *Civilizations in World Politics: Plural and Pluralist Perspectives*, Routledge.

Keohane, Robert O. (ed.) 1986 *Neo-realism and its Critics,* Columbia University Press.

Kepel, Gilles 2004 *The War for Muslim Minds: Islam and the West,* Belknap Press.

Khalizad, Zalmay and Daniel Byman 2000 'Afghanistan: The Consolidation of a Rogue State', *The Washington Quarterly*, Vol. 23, No. 1, pp. 65-78.

Khan, Sartaj 2009 'Imperialism, Religion and Class in Swat', *International Socialism,* No. 123. Available at http://www.isj.org.uk/index.php4?id=554&issue=123

Klimburg, Max 2001 'The Situation in Nuristan', *Central Asian Survey*, Vol. 20, No. 3, pp. 383-390.

Kochler, Hans 1993 *Democracy and the New World Order*: *Studies in International Relations,* XIX, International Progress Organization.

Kochler, Hans 2004 'Civilization as Instrument of World Order?: The Role of the Civilizational Paradigm in the Absence of a Balance of Power' Available at http://i-p-o.org/Koechler-Civilization_as_Instrument_of_World_Order-2006.pdf

Kristol, William and Robert Kagan October 29, 2001 'The Gathering Storm', *The Weekly Standard*, pp. 13-14.

Kung, Hans 1999 ' Inter- Cultural Dialogue Versus Confrontation' in Schmiegleow, Henrik (ed.) *Preventing the Clash of Civilizations: A Peace Strategy for the Twenty- First Century,* St. Martin's Press.

Kuran, Timur January/February 2011 'West is Best?', *Foreign Affairs,* Vol. 90, pp. 159-163.

Kurth, James 2001 'American and the West: Global Triumph or Western Twilight ?', *Orbis*, pp. 333-341.

Laclau, Ernest and Mouffe, Chantal 1985 *Hegemony and Socialist Strategy: Towards a Radical Democratic Politics,* Verso, pp.192-193.

Laclau, Ernest and Mouffe Chantal 1987 'Post-Marxism without Apologies', *New Left Review*. Available at http://sites.google.com/site/sgboehm/laclau-mouffe-nlr.pdf.

Laing, Ronald D. 1967 *The Politics of Experience,* Ballantine.

Lakshman, Narayan May 3, 2011 'U. S. Forces Kill Osama bin Laden', *The Hindu.*

Lansford, Tom and Jack Covarrubias 2003 'Osama bin Laden, Radical Islam and the United States' in Hayden, Patrick, Lansford, Tom and Watson, Robert P. (eds.) *America's War on Terror,* Ashgate.

Lehrer, Keith 2000 *Theory of Knowledge,* Westview Press.

Leonard, Stephen T. 1990 *Critical Theory in Political Practice,* Princeton.

Levitt, Zola 2005 *Dateline Jerusalem,* New Leaf Publishing Group.

Lewis, Bernard September 1990 'The Roots of Muslim Rage: Why so many Muslims Deeply Resent the West and Why Their Bitterness Will Not be Easily Mollified', *The Atlantic Monthly,* Vol. 266, No. 3, pp 47-58.

Linklater, Andrew 1990 *Beyond Marxism and Realism: Critical Theory and International Relations*, Macmillan.

Linklater, Andrew 1992 'The Question of the Next Stage in International Relations Theory', *Millennium*, Vol.21, No.1, pp. 77-98.

Linklater, Andrew 1992 'What is a Good International Citizen?' in Paul Keal (ed.) *Ethics and Foreign Policy*, Allen and Unwin, p. 21-43.

Linklater, Andrew 1996 'The Achievements of Critical Theory', in S. Smith, K. Booth and M. Zalewski (eds.) *International Theory: Positivism and Beyond,* Cambridge.

Linklater, Andrew and Scott Burchill (eds.) 1996 *Theories of International Relations,* Macmillan.

Linklater, Andrew 1998 *The Transformation of Political Community,* Columbia.

Linklater, Andrew 1998 *The Transformation of Political Community: Ethical Foundations of the Post-Westphalian Era,* University of South Carolina Press.

Linklater, Andrew 2000 'Men and Citizens in International Relations' in Andrew Linklater (ed.) *International Relations: Critical Concepts in Political Science,* Vol. 5, Routledge.

Linklater, Andrew 2000 *International Relations: Critical Concepts in Political Science,* Volume 4, Routledge.

Linklater, Andrew 2006 'The Harm Principle and Global Ethics', *Global Society,* Vol. 20, No. 3, pp.329-343.

Linklater, Andrew and Hidemi Suganami 2006 *The English School of International Relations: A Contemporary Reassessment,* Cambridge.

Linklater, Andrew 2007 *Critical Theory and World Politics: Citizenship, Sovereignty and Humanity*, Routledge.

Linklater, Andrew 2008 *Critical Theory and World Politics: Citizenship, Sovereignty and Humanity,* Manohar.

Lockwood, Jonathan 2010 'How Do the Three Major Ethnic Groups in Afghanistan Perceive the Conflict Led by the U.S. and NATO, their Future in Afghanistan, and their Courses of Action?'. Available at http://www.lamp-method.org/eCommons/Sheets.pdf.

Lowy, Michael 1996 *The War of Gods: Religion and Politics in Latin America*, Verso.

Luhmann, Niklas 1997 'Limits of Steering', *Theory, Culture and Society* , Vol.14, No.1, pp.41-57.

Lynch, Marc 2006 *Voices of the New Arab Public: Iraq, Al-Jazeera and Middle East Politics Today*, Columbia.

Lyotard 1984 *The Post-Modern Condition: A Report on Knowledge*, University of Minnesota Press.

Maaroof, Mohammad Khalid 1987 *Afghanistan in World Politics*, Gian Publishing House.

Magnus, Ralph H. and Naby, Eden 2000 *Afghanistan: Mullah, Marx and Mujahid*, Westview Press.

Mahbubani, Kishore 1992 'The West and the Rest', *National Interest,* Issue 28, pp. 10-14.

Maslow, A. 1965 'A Philosophy of Psychology' in Severin, F. (ed.) *Humanistic Viewpoints in Psychology,* McGraw Hill.

Marx, Karl 1852 *The Eighteenth Brumaire of Louis Bonaparte*. Available at http://www.marxists.org/archive/marx/works/1852/18th-brumaire/ch01.htm

McCarthy, T. 1978 *The Critical Theory of Jürgen Habermas*, Cambridge.

McGregor, Andrew 2003 'Jihad and the Rifle Alone: Abdullah Azzam and the Islamist Revolution', *The Journal of Conflict Studies*, Vol 23, No. 2. Available at https://journals.lib.unb.ca/index.php/jcs/article/view/219/377

Mildarsky, Manus I. 1998 'Democracy and Islam: Implication for Civilization Conflict and the Democratic Peace', *International Studies Quarterly*, Vol. 42, No. 3, pp. 485-511.

Millon, Theodore 2003 *Handbook of Psychology: Personality and Social Psychology*, Volume 5, Wiley.

Mintz, Elianna August 31, 2011 '9/11 Commission Warns U.S. Still Vulnerable 10 Years After Attacks', *The Talk Radio News Service.*

Monshipouri, Mahmood and Gina Petonito 1995 'Constructing the Enemy in the Post- Cold War Era: The Flaws of the Islamic Conspiracy Theory', *Journal of Church and State*, Vol. 37, No. 4, pp. 773-792.

Monsutti, Alessandro 2005 *War and Migration: Social Networks and Economic Strategies of the Hazaras of Afghanistan* (translated by Patrick Camiller), Routledge.

Mousavi, Sayed Askar 1997 *The Hazaras of Afghanistan: An Historical, Cultural, Economic and Political Study,* St. Martin's Press.

Murphy, Craig 1994 *International Organization and Industrial Change*, Cambridge.

Norris, Pippa and Ronald Inglehart April 2002 'Islam and the West: Testing the Clash of Civilizations Thesis', John F. Kennedy School of Government, *Harvard University Faculty Research Working Papers Series* (RW PO 2-015).

Olesen, Asta 1996 *Islam and Politics in Afghanistan*, Curzon Press.

Ottaway, Marina and Anatol Lievan 2002 'Rebuilding Afghanistan: Fantasy versus Reality', *Peace Initiatives*, Vol. 3, Nos. 1-3, pp. 127-144.

Ozcel_K, Sezai 2005 'Neorealist and Neo-Gramscian Hegemony in International Relations and Conflict Resolution During the 1990's'. Available at http://dergipark.ulakbim.gov.tr/esad/article/viewFile/1068000023/1068000147

Pavlov, Ivan 1941 'Lectures on Conditioned Reflexes', Vol. 2: *Conditioned Reflexes and Psychiatry* translated and edited by W.H. Gantt, Lawrence and Wishart Ltd. Available at http://s-f-walker.org.uk/pubsebooks/pdfs/Condditioned%20Reflexes%20And%20Psychiatry.pdf

Payne, Rodger A. 2000 'Habermas, Discourse Norms, and the Prospects for Global Deliberation', 41ˢᵗ Annual Convention of International Studies Association, Los Angeles, California.

Peimani, Hooman 2003 *Falling Terrorism and Rising Conflict,* Prager.

Piven, Jerry S. 2002 'On the Psychosis (Religion) of Terrorists' in Stout, Chris E. (ed.) *The Psychology of Terrorism* Vol. III, Praeger, pp 119-140.

Polanyi, Karl 2010 *The Great Transformation: The Political and Economic Origins of Our Time,* Beacon Press.

Postone, Moishe 1993 *Time, Labor and Social Domination: A Reinterpretation of Marx's Critical Theory,* Cambridge.

Price, Richard and Christian Reus-Smit 1998 'Dangerous Liaisons? Critical International Theory and Constructivism', *European Journal of International Relations,* Vol.4, No. 3, pp. 259-294.

Pugh, Michael Charles, Neil Cooper and Jonathan Goodhand 2004 *War Economies in a Regional Context: Challenges of Transformation*, Lynne Rienner Publishers.

Rashid, Ahmed November/December, 1999 'Taliban: Exporting Extremism', *Foreign Affairs,* Vol.78, No. 6, pp. 22-35.

Rashid, Ahmed 2001 'Afghanistan: Ending the Policy Quagmire', *Journal of International Affairs,* Vol.54, No.2, pp. 395-410.

Rashid, Ahmed 2001 *Taliban: Militant Islam, Oil and Fundamentalism in Central Asia,* Yale University Press.

Rasuly-Paleczek, Gabriele 1998 'Ethnic Identity versus Nationalism: The Uzbeks of North-Eastern Afghanistan and the Afghan State' in Atabaki, Touraj and O'Kane, John (eds.), *Post-Soviet Central Asia*, Tauris Academic Studies.

Rasuly-Paleczek, Gabriele 2001 'The Struggle for the Afghan State: Centralization, Nationalism and their Discontents' in Schendel, Willem Van and Zurcher, Erik J. (eds.) *Identity Politics in Central Asia and the Muslim World: Nationalism, Ethnicity and Labour in the Twentieth Century*, I.B. Tauris Publishers.

RAWA, 'Shoulder to Shoulder, Hand in Hand: Resistance Under the Iron Fist in Afghanistan´, Winter 2002 *Radical History Review,* Issue 82, pp.131-140.

Richard Rosecrance December 1998 'The book review of the Clash of Civilizations and the Remaking of World Order', *American Political Science Review*, Vol. 92, No. 4, p978-980.

Robert Marks 2002 'The book review of The Clash of Civilizations and the Remaking of World Order', *Journal of World History,* Vol. 11, No.1, pp101-104.

Robinson, William I. 2004 *A Theory of Global Capitalism: Production Class and the State in a Transnational World*, John Hopkins University Press.

Rogers, C.R. 1961 *On Becoming a Person*, Houghton Miffline.

Rosenberg, Justin 1994 *The Empire of Civil Society*, Verso.

Rosenberg, Justin, 2000, *The Follies of Globalization Theory,* Verso.

Roy, Oliver October, 1989 'Afghanistan Back to Tribalism or on to Lebanon?', *Third World Quarterly*, Vol. 11, No.4, pp. 70-82.

Roy, Oliver 1995 *Afghanistan from Holy War to Civil War*, Darwin Press.

Roy, Oliver 1995 *The Failure of Political Islam*, Cambridge University Press.

Roy, Oliver 2004 *Globalized Islam: The Search for a New Ummah,* Hurst and Company.

Rubenstein, Richard E. and Jarle Crocker 1994 'Challenging Huntington', *Foreign Policy*, No. 96, pp. 115-117.

Rubin, Barnett R. 1999 'The Political Economy of War and Peace in Afghanistan'. Available at http://citeseerx.ist.psu.edu/viewdoc/download?doi=10.1.1.461.517&rep=rep1&type=pdf

Rubin, Trudy February 19, 2009 'Taming the Good Taliban'. Available at http://www.realclearworld.com/articles/2009/02/taming_the_good_taliban_afpak.html

Russet, Bruce, John R. O'Neal and Michealene Cox September 2002 'Clash of Civilizations or Realism and Liberalism Deja Vu? Some Evidence', *Journal of Peace Research*, Vol. 378, No. 5, pp 583-608.

Said, Edward W. October, 22, 2001 'The Clash of Ignorance', *The Nation.* Available at http://www.bintjbeil.com/articles/en/011018_omayma.html

Saikal, Amin and William Maley 1991 *Regime Change in Afghanistan: Foreign Intervention and the Politics of Legitimacy*, Westview Press.

Saikal, Amin 2006 *Modern Afghanistan: A History of Struggle and Survival*, I. B. Tauris.

Sarat, Austin 2011 Special Issue: New Possibilities/New Problems, Volume 56 of Studies in Law, Politics and Society Series, Emerald Group Publishing.

Sardar, Ziauddin and Merryl Wyn Davies 2004 *American Dream, Global Nightmare,* Cambridge.

Sato, Seizaburo October 1997 'The Clash of Civilizations: A View from Japan', *Asia Pacific Review* 4, pp. 7-23.

Selby, Jan 2007 'Engaging Foucault: Discourse, Liberal Governance, and the Limits of Foucauldian IR', *International Relations,* Vol. 21, No. 3, pp. 324-345.

Shah, Sardar Ikbal Ali 1978 *Afghanistan of the Afghans*, Re-print Gosha-e-Adab.

Shahzad, Syed Saleem October 25, 2003 'Pashtunistan Issue back to Haunt Pakistan', *Asia Times.* Available at http://www.atimes.com/atimes/South_Asia/EJ25Df01.html

Shapcott, Richard 2001 *Justice, Community and Dialogue in International Relations,* Cambridge University Press.

Shaw, Martin 2000 *Theory of the Global State: Globality as an Unfinished Revolution*, Cambridge University Press.

Sheridan, Michael November 1, 1998 'How the Taliban Slaughtered Thousands of People', *The Sunday Times.* Available at http://www.rawa.org/times.htm

Shibley Telhani Conference, May 14-15, 2002, 'The United States, Europe and the Muslim World: Revitalizing Relations after September 11', *CSIS: Islam Program,* Washington D.C.

Shirkogoroff, S. M. 1935 *Psychomental Complex of the Tungus*, Kegan Paul, Trench, Trubner.

Singh, Amar Kumar December 1998 'The Concept of Man in Psychology', *Social Change,* Vol.28, No.4, pp. 1-35.

Sinno, Abdulkader H. 2008 *Organizations at War in Afghanistan and Beyond*, Cornell University Press.

Sohail, Khalid 2010 'Muslims, Quran and the 21st Century'. Available at http://www.cobourgatheist.com/index.php?option=com_content&view=article&id=771:muslims-quran-and-the-21st-century&catid=17&Itemid=60

Sterling-Folker, Jennifer 2008 'Postmodern and Critical Theory Approaches' in Jennifer Sterling-Folker (ed.) *Making Sense of International Relations Theory,* Lynne Reinner Publishers.

Stirling, Mack, C. 2007 'Violent Religion: Rene Girard's Theory of Culture' in Ellens, J. Harold (ed.) *Destructive Power of Religion, Vol.2: Religion, Psychology and Violence,* pp. 11-50.

Strachey, J.(ed.) 1968 *The Standard Edition of the Complete Psychological Works of Sigmund Freud* Vol.21, Hogarth Press, pp. 59-148.

Sutton, Philip W. and Stephen Vertigans 2005 *Resurgent Islam: A Sociological Approach,* Polity.

Szasz, T.S. 1960 'The Myth of Mental Illness', *American Psychologist*, Vol. 15, pp 113-118.

Teschke, Benno 2003 *The Myth of 1648*, Verso.

Turner, Jonathan 1998 'Must Sociological Theory and Sociological Practice Be So Far Apart?: A Polemical Answer', *Sociological Perspectives,* Vol. 41, pp.243-258.

United Nations Office on Drugs and Crime, 2003 'The Opium Economy of Afghanistan'. Available at http://www.unodc.org/pdf/publications/afg_opium_economy_www.pdf

Urban, Mark 1990 *War in Afghanistan,* Palgrave Macmillan.

Vanaik, Achin 1997 *The Furies of Indian Communalism: Religion, Modernity and Secularization,* Verso.

Vanaik, Achin 2004 'US Perspectives in a Global and South Asian Context: Before and After 11 September' in Haidar, Salman (ed.) *The Afghan War and its Geopolitical Implications for India,* Manohar.

Vanaik, Achin 2007 *Masks of Empire.* Tulika Books.

Vanaik, Achin 24-30 April, 2010 'The Issue of Nuclear Terrorism', *Economic and Political Weekly,* Vol. 45, No. 17, pp. 10-13.

Volkman, Ernest 2002 *Science Goes to War: The Search for the Ultimate Weapon, from Greek Fire to Star Wars*, Wiley.

Wasim, Naz 2001 'Challenging Samuel Huntington's The Clash of Civilizations: The Shared Tradition of Europe, and Islam' in International Conference on the Dialogue of Civilizations. Available at http://www.unu.edu/dialogue/conf-report.pdf

Wedgwood, Ruth 2002 'Al Qaeda, Terrorism and Military Commissions', *American Journal of International Law,* Vol. 96, No. 2, pp. 328-337.

Will, George September 11, 2011 '9/11, Wars Leave the US Feeling Vulnerable', *Newsmax*. Available at http://www.newsmax.com/GeorgeWill/9-11-iraq/2011/09/11/id/410468

Williams, Raymond 1981 *Culture,* Fontana Press.

Zeidan, David 2001 'The Islamic Fundamentalist View of Life as a Perennial Battle'. Available at http://www.rubincenter.org/2001/12/zeidan-htm-2001-12-02/

Zimbardo, Philip G. 2004 'A Situationist Perspective on the Psychology of Evil' in Miller, Arthur G.(ed.) *The Social Psychology of Good and Evil,* Guilford Publications.

Note on Indexing

E-IR's publications do not feature indexes due to the prohibitive costs of assembling them. If you are reading this book in paperback and want to find a particular word or phrase you can do so by downloading a free PDF version of this book from the E-IR website.

View the e-book in any standard PDF reader such as Adobe Acrobat Reader (pc) or Preview (mac) and enter your search terms in the search box. You can then navigate through the search results and find what you are looking for. In practice, this method can prove much more targeted and effective than consulting an index.

If you are using apps (or devices) such as iBooks or Kindle to read our e-books, you should also find word search functionality in those.

You can find all of our e-books at: http://www.e-ir.info/publications

www.ingramcontent.com/pod-product-compliance
Lightning Source LLC
Chambersburg PA
CBHW050732030426
42336CB00012B/1526